MASTERING
THE TABLES OF
TIME

by David Stanoch

Foreword by **Elliot Fine**

Music Engraving by **Mark Powers**

Layout and Back Cover Photo by **Katy Tessman Stanoch**

Online Companion Recording, Mixing & Mastering by:
Jeff Peterson and **David Stanoch**
at **Studio Rhythmelodic**, Minnetonka, MN

DISTRIBUTED BY:
Alfred Music Publishing Co., Inc.
P.O. Box 10003
Van Nuys, CA 91410-0003

PUBLISHED BY:
RHYTHMELODIC MUSIC
© 2008 Rhythmelodic Music, Second Edition

VOLUME I

Introducing
the Standard
Timetable

Table of Contents
Mastering the Tables of Time ~ Volume I

Foreword

When David Stanoch began studying with me many years ago, I could see that he had the potential, desire and determination to become a great drummer. I have since then seen him blossom into a first-class drummer, producer, clinician, teacher, and now, author.

David is constantly absorbing and learning from all available sources, styles and concepts of drumming, from the past to the future, to create his own voice.

I sincerely recommend *Mastering the Tables of Time* to any drummer wanting a strong foundation to play the complex styles and coordination of the future. It's all here and the concepts are timeless. In my estimation it is the most exciting and challenging book to come out in years.

Congratulations David. It is a truly monumental work. You have my love, respect and admiration.

Elliot Fine
Percussionist,
Minnesota Orchestra (retired)
Co-author of *4-Way Coordination*

Preface

The studies in this book uniquely combine the foundations of rhythm and the foundations of trapset drumming using a common system to assimilate the disciplines of timekeeping, coordination, rudiments, polyrhythms, and musical phrasing. The table of time provides an inclusive framework for combining these exclusive areas of study to benefit players of any skill level, be it beginner, intermediate, or advanced, with an interest in developing a musical foundation with crystal-clear focus for complete freedom of expression in any direction.

It is said there is nothing new under the sun, and applying the table of time to improve one's rhythmic sensibilities is certainly nothing new. I've studied excellent applications by Joe Morello, Andrew Cyrille, Gary Chaffee, Marvin Dahlgren and Elliot Fine that were all very effective in their purpose. There are others as well. Developing a comprehensive method of study around its foundation evolved gradually. My curiosity about its possibilities was piqued in 1997, after reading this quote from Tony Williams:

"It's all in time. Don't do things faster; faster doesn't get you anywhere. You have to play in time, in context. Pick a meter and play it, double it then triple it. Do it in eighth-note triplets, sixteenth-notes, sixteenth-note triplets, thirty-second notes, thirty-second note triplets. Don't play arbitrarily faster or slower. It has to be in time. The goal is to play clearly. If you don't, you're not expressing yourself; you're not playing something that people can hear. When I first recorded myself...I realized you have to play things that are clear to you so they will be clear to somebody else."

Examples of phrases Tony used on *his* drumset blew my mind when I played through them on *mine* using the method he described! For me, something clicked. This was a conceptually inspirational lesson and for the next ten years I explored further uses for the table of time and was amazed at the greater dimension it gave my playing. Along the way, I began to suspect that this focus of study was a lost art–a missing link commonly handed down back in the days before the so-called "self taught" ideology evolved with the garage band craze of the 1960's, creating a disconnect in certain areas of musical development that are only now coming back into vogue.

Consider Jo Jones who on his 1973 recording, "The Drums," refers to the timetables almost offhandedly, when discussing "essentials" for drummers, as if *everyone* knew how important they were for building their foundation. Tony Williams certainly understood what Jo was talking about. My suspicion lit a fire to master the tables of time with a progressive approach that reached farther musically than I'd seen it taken before. So, as Elliot Fine had taught me as a child, I applied my imagination to its structure, and suddenly everything I threw at it seemed to stick (no pun intended). The results were inspiring.

Over time I shared some of my discoveries with a handful of highly respected drummers who were impressed with the concept and its benefits and enthusiastically encouraged me to continue its development. That is when the focus shifted from my personal study to one that could be musically beneficial to all, on many levels, without bells, whistles or jive.

In setting the highest standard for a unifying, yet multi-directional function, I kept the teaching methods of Alan Dawson in mind as the benchmark, as they address several important aspects of playing musically all at once–just as we do in performance. For those of you not familiar with Alan (who taught a young Tony Williams, and whom I also had the great privilege to study with), or his methods, refer to *Selected Media for Further Study* (pg.139) and check them out for yourself.

The foundation attainable using the *Standard Timetable* is plentiful and rich. A philosophy I've adapted in my course of study, that I believe has value in sharing, is that while drummers often describe the rudiments as "our scales," I've come to see them simply as part of our vocabulary–like words that need context to create sentences or phrases. I see the *subdivisions* as our scales–the *rhythm scale*, as the timetable is sometimes called. An immediate revelation for forming those "sentences" are the phrasing *alternatives* that springs to life as you move *any* accent pattern, rudiment, polyrhythm, or groove of your choice through the timetable. This understanding breeds great clarity for making musical choices. You can see and hear unified rhythmic relationships that may have once seemed disparate or unrelated. This is particularly true of the polyrhythm studies. This knowledge immediately expands your soloing vocabulary and most certainly will strengthen your groove and timekeeping overall.

Remember that good timekeeping is an important component of any serious musician's skill set. Every musician should have a strong sense of time but for a drummer it is absolutely essential because, in our primary role as an accompanist, it is expected as our foundation. A drummer today must be able to groove both in organic *real-time*, and also in inorganic *quantized* time. To develop a feel for these disciplines, one important concept to consider is that they are largely defined by how you use the *space* between the beats. The space needs the same focus and attention as the notes you are playing. Time and space working in harmony will affect *how* you'll play those notes in a way that will smooth out your time flow, providing a deeper *feel* for the music you play.

While it is essential to have good time, it is only *one* aspect of our overall musicality. Vocabulary, color, shading, and imagination are also important to the *interpretation* of the music we play. These nuances are all present in any well-seasoned drummer's *timekeeping* as well. Having this awareness of *nuance* and the ability to apply it is, in my opinion, what separates a truly great drummer from the others who simply "play the drums." These studies promote this awareness and promise a new confidence and conviction in your playing that you can carry into any musical scenario you choose.

Volume I is a virtual reference library on the foundations of rhythm and trapset drumming as it was originally conceived in the USA, combining European rudiments, African polyrhythms, 4-way coordination, jazz and backbeat grooves, and soloing vocabulary, to create a new sound in music. *Volume II* will advance the study as the focus goes global, introducing the asymmetric groupings of the *World Timetable*, and incorporating rhythms of Pan-African, Indian, and related cultures, into the *Standard* and *World Timetable* frameworks. Abstract phrasing studies and other surprises await! Enjoy the journey.

Acknowledgement

Inspiration for this work has come from precedent set in lessons, conversations, and the works and musical performances of Elliot Fine, Marvin Dahlgren, Richard Davis, Alan Dawson, Tony Williams, Max Roach, Art Blakey, Elvin Jones, Joe Morello, Andrew Cyrille, Ed Blackwell, Phil Hey, Jeff "Tain" Watts, Eric Kamau Gravatt, Gordy Knudtson, Jeff Hamilton, Ignacio Berroa, Bernard Purdie, John Vidacovich, Stanton Moore, Ari Hoenig, Gary Chaffee, Terry Bozzio, Chad Wackerman, Vinnie Colaiuta, Steve Smith, and Peter Erskine. Each motivated me, in different ways, to develop and expand the application of the table of time into broader directions. I salute you all.

Some special notes of thanks, first to Gordy Knudtson, who, by example, has always inspired me to diversify in my professional activities, and provided me a wonderful career opportunity to develop and exercise my knowledge. The encouragement and enthusiasm Gordy extended to me after hearing my concepts was my primary motivation for writing this book. In other words: no Gordy, no book. Thank you always Gordy for believing in me. Your friendship and support have been a bedrock to my family.

Next, to Elliot Fine: I love you, Elliot. I owe you so much. Thank you for sharing your knowledge, experience, humor, and selfless friendship. Where would I be without you and all of your great encouragement for all these years? So many great opportunities have come my way because of my relationship with you. Thank you for pushing me to the finish line with this project, and offering to write the Foreword. I am honored.

To Marvin Dahlgren, one of the finest gentlemen I've ever had the pleasure to know and whose restless musical mind is an inspiration to us all. It has been a true privilege to work along side you both at the McNally Smith College of Music and on countless bandstands for so many years. Thank you for your friendship and support, it inspires me.

I want especially recognize both Richard Davis–for his mentoring, love, providing great opportunities for us to play together, and for teaching me how to find tempos using my wristwatch–and Phil Hey, for more invaluable mentoring and love, selflessly providing me my first gig experiences, and for always, always being there for me. Nobody swings like you my friends. Thanks for everything.

To Alan Dawson and Max Roach for their legacies and for sharing with me, as they did for so many, the keys to truly musical drumming. Thank you gentlemen.

Many thanks also to Ignacio Berroa, Jeff Hamilton, Bernard Purdie, and John Vidacovich, who all offered great encouragement and advice to enhance the potential they saw in my ideas. You are all marvelous. Thanks for your inspiration.

Thanks also to my friends, Kevin Daley and Jeff Peterson for their expertise, advice and assistance in helping me realize the online audio and video companion resources for the book.

Lastly, I wish to express my gratitude to my dear friend, the late George Tucker, who was invaluable in first helping me get the book together. Thanks Tuck. I miss you.

About Mark Powers

I met Mark Powers when he came to the McNally Smith College of Music (then Musictech) at age sixteen for an audition. He'd graduated early from high school and was serious about "this drumming thing." He played well that day and excelled through our program. After graduating he hit the road playing around the world with "America's Polka King," Frankie Yankovic. Not long after that he was playing with Cheap Trick's Rick Neilsen, (Now that's versatility!) An eternal student, Mark has traveled to China, Thailand, and West Africa to pursue studies in percussion and has also studied with Dane Richeson, Bob Moses, and Ed Thigpen.

A true self-starter, Mark is currently in too many bands, has too many drum students, is often an Artist-in-Residence at area elementary, middle and high schools, conducts 'Junk Jam' workshops, teaches West African drumming, and presents percussion-based Correctional Education programs in adult and juvenile facilities. Mark has written for PAS Percussive Notes, and World Percussion & Rhythm magazines, and Drummer's Digest, and World Rhythm Web-zines. A published composer of percussion works, he also holds a shared Guinness World Record for Longest Drum Roll by a Group.

As busy as you can see that he is, Mark agreed to take on the job of helping me organize my endless scribbling into the book before you. He worked tirelessly on the music engraving and layout, helped with text editing, offered great feedback, and was a true confidant throughout the project. I got the guy I wanted and I think we both learned a lot in the process. Thank you Mark for your friendship, talent and true commitment. It is greatly appreciated.

Visit www.powerspercussion.com.

Dedication

This work is dedicated to my family: my beautiful wife Katy, and wonderful children, Louis and Maxwell, for the faith they have in me and the strength and sense of purpose it gives me. To my dear mother and father, Lois and Bruno, for the love, opportunity, and support they provided me to develop and nurture my passion for music. To my brother John, for sharing his love of music with me when we were children. And to my wonderful mother-in-law and father-in-law, Charon and Bill Tessman, who have shown my family selfless love and support and provided me a peaceful haven to develop many of the ideas presented herein. I am forever grateful to you all.

David Stanoch

Audio/Video Online Resource Information

Audio and video demonstrations from each chapter of *Mastering the Tables of Time, Volume I,* as well as exclusive Web-only PDF file examples, are available for FREE online at:

www.rhythmelodic.com

The audio, video, and printable resources available on the Web site serve as a means to *hear* and *see* the concepts presented in the book. A major benefit of presenting material online is that it can be fluid and ongoing in nature, incorporating updates and variations. The foundations of the *Standard* and *World Timetables,* as well as the *Abstract "Syncopated Standard,"* and *"Dotted Subdivision" Timetables,* are clearly presented and also expanded on in ways that tie all the chapter concepts together, just as one would want to do when performing.

Many of these examples incorporate sticking, voicing, and ostinato variations, recommended in the *Practice Tips* section of each chapter of the book, for "getting off the page" and into greater musical expression.

Click Tracks

In practice, each section of any timetable should be played repeatedly, until it is comfortable in time, feel and dynamic balance, before going on to the next section. The use of a metronome is highly recommended for building a strong foundation in timekeeping. It is equally important to practice the same ideas without one with a focus on internalizing the feeling of the tempo.

A variety of click tracks are also downloadable at the Web site for accompaniment in practicing all of the timetables. The click track examples focus on Largo to Adagio (slow) Tempi, from 40-60 bpm, to build a strong foundation for *all* subdivisions presented, and Andante through Moderato to Allegretto (moderately slow to moderately fast) Tempi, from 72-120 bpm, as common tempo applications for all timetables.

Also available are "Polyclicks"– which provide two pulses and tempos simultaneously (primarily for use with *Chapter 5, Basic Polyrhythms & Hemiola Part Two: Combination & Coordination Studies*). With these clicks you can apply timetables to "either side" of 3:2 or 2:3, and 3:4 or 4:3 polyrhythms.

For *Chapters 6 (Contemporary Backbeat Grooves)* and *7 (Modern Jazz Grooves)* the use of play-along CDs, with bass lines or full rhythm section in a variety of groove styles, is recommended to find "the pocket" for the groove studies presented within. Bass lines employ both the *attack* and *release* of the notes (vs. the *attack-only* function of a click). Practicing in this manner better informs the drummer in how to *steer* the direction of the time (see *Preface*, pg. *iv*) on the bandstand or in the studio. *"Any drummer can have a good beat. It takes at least two people to create a groove."* ~ Johnny Vidacovich.

Notation Guide

Reading Music

A basic understanding of reading music is required to fully absorb the studies. Refer to *Selected Media for Further Study* (pg. 139) to find recommended texts for reading development. Those still developing their reading skills can access audio and video recordings of many of the examples (see pg. *viii*) to *hear* and *see* them being played. Whatever your level of reading skill, remember that *hearing* the music helps you to "get off the page" and absorb the *feeling* for it. Reading music seems as important to me as being able to read *any* language we speak. Where would you be if you couldn't? Knowledge is power, so empower yourself! Finding a teacher who inspires you is also very helpful in this regard.

Notation Key and Staff Variations

To provide the most universal option in presenting the studies in this book, the drumset voicing is based loosely around a standard "four-piece" configuration of the instrument (as played by a right-handed drummer): bass drum (with double bass drum or pedal optional), snare drum, one mounted tom, one floor tom, hi-hat, left and right side suspended cymbals, and a cowbell. Left-handed players should simply reverse all stickings for hands and feet. Motives written for double bass drums can also be played with single bass drum and vice versa. Experiment.

Four types of staff notation are employed in various sections of the book, each best suited to the studies they focus on. They are illustrated below, along with a key included for the type of notation used in conjunction with them. *Example 1* is a one-line version of "Swiss notation." This staff outlines the sticking by placing notes in the right hand *above* the line and notes for the left hand *below*.

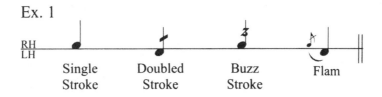

Example 2 is a two-line version of "Swiss notation." This staff adds the "sticking" for the feet on the lower line, placing bass drum notes in the right foot *above* the bottom line and hi-hat or second bass drum notes for the left foot *below* the bottom line.

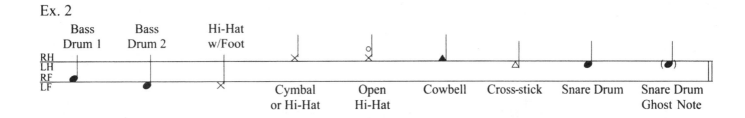

There will be examples of "neutralized sticking" placed directly *on* the lines of the one and two-line staves when more than one sticking option is preferable and will be so noted in the text.

Example 3 is a three-line "Swiss notation" variation. The top and bottom lines function the same as the two-line staff, and the middle line illustrates a rhythm that should be applied to more than one voice, like snare drum and bass drum, for example.

Ex. 3

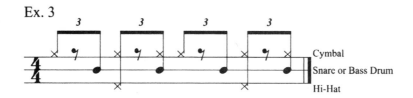

Example 4 is a standard five-line staff, neutral in clef. This staff is used for soloing examples containing mounted and floor tom voicing, in addition to bass drum, snare drum and cymbals, to illustrate *visually* the melodic contour of the phrases. The sticking, in these examples, is indicated underneath the first two measures of each timetable and remains consistent as the subdivisions double or triple, respectively.

Ex. 4

16th Note Triplet vs. Sextuplet Phrasing

In order to maximize the emphasis on the double and triple-time phrasing relationship of all 16th and 32nd note subdivisions of the *Standard Timetable* to their 8th note counterparts, all 16th note *triplets* in this volume are subdivided as one 16th note triplet per 8th note, as seen below in *Example 1*, versus the flow of the sextuplet, based on the foundation of an 8th note triplet subdivided into 16th notes, as seen below in *Example 2*. (32nd triplet subdivisions then follow the same model over 16th notes)

Ex. 1   Ex. 2

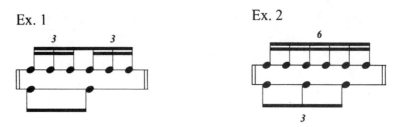

There is, or can be, an implied variation of *feel* with the difference in notation. In looking at *Example 1*, imagine the sound of two *8th* *note* triplets in a bar of 2/4 time. In looking at Example 2, imagine the sound of three groups of *8th notes* in a bar of 3/4 time. Apply those feels to the *sixteenth* subdivisions above and there you have it. The sextuplet variation will be integrated fully into the *World Timetable* studies in *Volume II* of *Mastering the Tables of Time*, but it is encouraged that you apply it to any examples of 16th note triplets in *Volume I* to experience the variety.

Final Notes on Text and Tempo

The purpose of categorizing the various timetables serves to highlight applications unique to each. The *Standard Timetable* expands and contracts motives into half, double, and triple-time feels. One timetable typically provides several tempo applications. In musical performance, keep in mind that the more "dense" subdivisions (like 16^{ths} and 32^{nds}) work best at slower tempos. The more spacious note values (half, quarter and 8th notes) are easier to play at faster tempos. Practice with a metronome for reference, to be sure you're locked in 100%, then play the same things again without one to help internalize the feeling. Do this at a variety of tempos. Record yourself and study the playbacks objectively, focusing on your time and feel.

The *Abstract Timetables* give "artistic license" for thinking "outside the box" of a common timetable structure, erasing limitations to provide greater musical possibilities. *The World Timetable* focuses on a gradual increase of subdivisions inside the foundation of a quarter-note pulse, from one to nine notes per beat, adding asymmetric grouping of five, seven, and nine into the fold. This offers a more advanced polyrhythmic flow to the various studies applied to it.

Each chapter begins with a bit of perspective on the topic of study. Recognizing *what* the function of any given subject is helps to understand *why* it is important. *How* to apply it to both our instrument and the "big picture" of music is covered in the *Applications* section. Each chapter text concludes with *Practice Tips* that offer food for thought for "getting off the page" and lighting the creative spark for developing your own musical vocabulary. That is the ultimate goal, I believe, for any type of study.

Introduction
The Standard Timetable Presented in Roundtable Form

The following page illustrates the *Standard Timetable* in *Roundtable Form* (see *Glossary of Terms*, pg. 135). Within a simple meter framework we will use five consecutive note value groupings for this timetable: half-notes, quarter-notes, eighth-notes, sixteenth-notes, and thirty-second notes, focusing on the duple and triple subdivisions common to each grouping. The goal is to be able to comfortably hear, anticipate and play musically through all of the note values while keeping steady time based on the quarter-note pulse.

Application

Begin by setting a metronome to a slow pulse of around 40 to 60 beats per minute. Try playing and singing the rhythms. Drummers typically execute only the attack of the notes and not their full duration when playing these rhythms. Singing the full duration of the notes helps you hear and feel the *release* of the note as well as the attack. This awareness is extremely helpful for understanding how important *space* is to produce a steady, "good feeling" flow of time.

Letters C and D are the quarter-note subdivisions. C flows at the same pulse as the time signature. Think of this pulse as the "root rhythm" (see *Glossary of Terms*, pg. 135), or foundation, that all the other subdivisions "spring from." The duple and triple rhythms are consistent, in their sound and feel relationships, to one another for each note value grouping. The subdivisions define the rate of speed they are played at.

Half-note subdivisions (A and B) then create a *half-time* pulse, flowing half as fast as the quarter-note pulse. 8th note subdivisions (E and F) create a *double-time* pulse, flowing twice as fast as the quarter-note pulse. 16th note subdivisions (G and H) create a *triple-time* pulse, flowing three times as fast as the quarter-note pulse. And finally the 32nd note subdivisions (I and J) create a *quadruple-time* pulse, flowing four times as fast as the quarter-note pulse. Letters K-S simply repeat subdivisions A-I in reverse order (illustrating the *Roundtable Form* concept).

Tempos vary widely in music. Mastering the timetable allows you to apply rhythmic phrasing to extremes in tempo. Try this: decrease the subdivisions by half while doubling the tempo, playing first 32nd groupings at 40 bpm, then 16^{ths} at 80 bpm, and finally 8^{ths} at 160 bpm. These combinations will sound identical in execution even though the tempos and subdivisions are different. This practical knowledge is useful for applying any examples in this book to musical phrasing at any tempo.

Practice Tips

How to count the subdivisions is entirely subjective. It is recommended, at first, to use the eighth-note count, as illustrated in Letters E and F, throughout all the respective duple and triple subdivisions. This gives you a mental common denominator for keeping the overall pulse steady. The bigger notes will flow together evenly; and you won't crowd your mind with every little note either. You can then focus on the big picture, allowing you and the rhythm to better breathe. Try it yourself, we're just getting started!

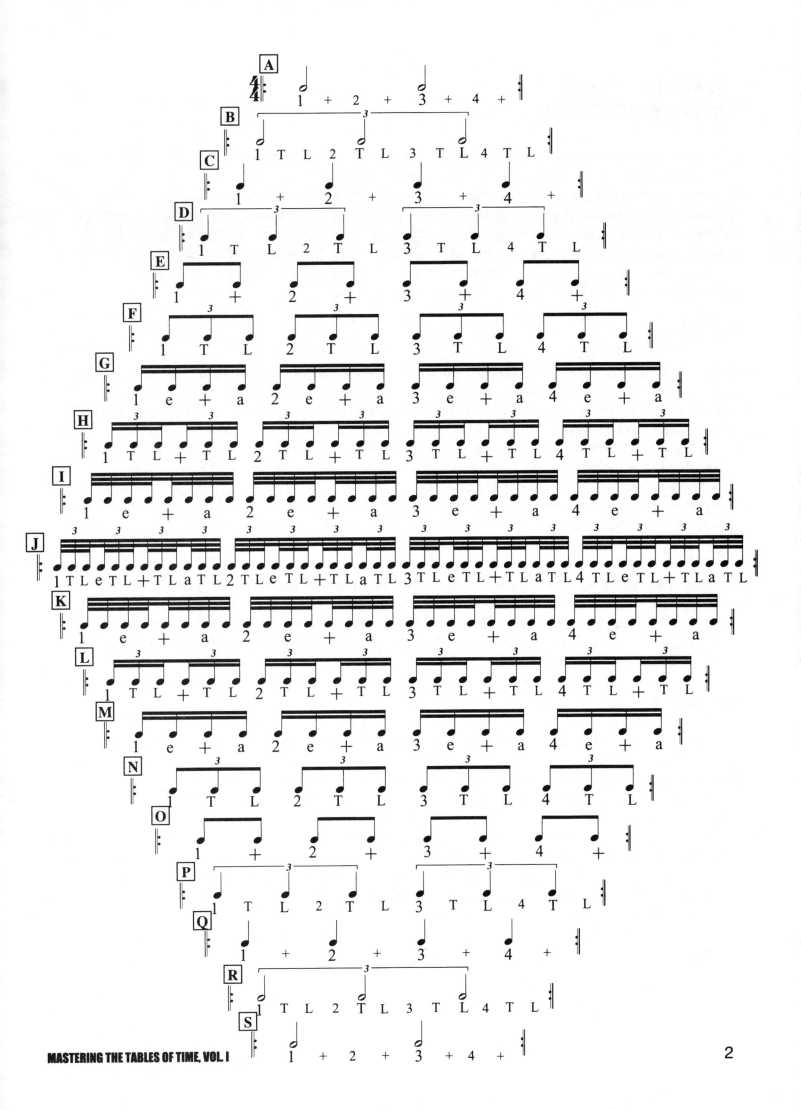

In developing your instrumental skills, complete musicality is the highest goal. A rhythm player must also think melodically and harmonically. Once you can play the basic subdivisions of the *Standard Timetable* comfortably and consistently at a variety of tempos, musical phrasing is the logical next step. Musical styles are defined by how the subdivisions within their rhythms are phrased to give the proper feeling to the music. The accent studies on the following pages address musical phrasing with broad stylistic applications to ensemble figures, soloing and grooving. By striking percussion in the execution of these rhythms we can also apply muted and open tone interpretation to the accented phrasing, allowing for great variance of pitch and melodic color in application.

Application

Part IA illustrates common sequenced groupings of accented and unaccented notes expressed in time signatures relative to the length of the phrase. In this section the phrases compress rhythmically as you increase the subdivisions in the bar and expand as you decrease them. Part IB illustrates a sampling of rhythmic motives common to many musical styles. The length of each phrase in Part IB is consistent per bar (or bars) as the subdivisions increase or decrease within it. Comparc Part IA, example 1 to Part IB, example 1, to see the difference.

The groupings in Part IA each begin with a foundational pattern accenting the downbeat of the measure (labeled as *Root Position*), followed by *inversions* of all possible rhythmic permutations, or displacements, for each grouping (see *Glossary of Terms*, pg. 135).

These *Accent Studies* also give us our first look at the use of polyrhythmic phrasing, so common in many musical styles. Observe how the *two* and *four-note* phrases in Part IA flow over the *triple* subdivisions (creating polyrhythms of 3:2 and 6:2, or 3:4 and 6:4) and how the *three-note* phrases flow over the *duple* subdivisions (creating polyrhythms of 2:3 and 4:3). Examples 6-9 in Part IB feature the use of *hemiola* (see *Glossary of Terms*, pg. 135), illustrating rhythmic motives that extend over bar lines.

Practice Tips

To more easily master the phrases, the sticking is written hand-to-hand. Playing the accented notes in one hand and the unaccented notes in the other is also recommended where practical. Use your imagination to interpret the exercises. Experiment with playing *only* the accented notes. Try muting or "*dead-sticking*" (using no rebound) the accented notes and playing the unaccented notes with open tones. Then do the reverse. The muted notes will be higher in pitch than the open tones, as openly accented notes are vs. unaccented ones, and provide a different melodic color with a slight pitch-bending effect. Various dynamic levels offer more variety of pitches. Play the examples at a variety of soft, moderate and loud dynamic levels. Doing this at a variety of tempos will greatly improve your control and sensitivity. You can apply the feet, playing them before, on, or after the accents, or using the *Counterpoint Ostinato Options* on pg. 25, etc.

Accent Studies ~ Part IA: Selected Common Sequenced Groupings

1. Two-Note Grouping: One Accented / One Unaccented (Root Position)

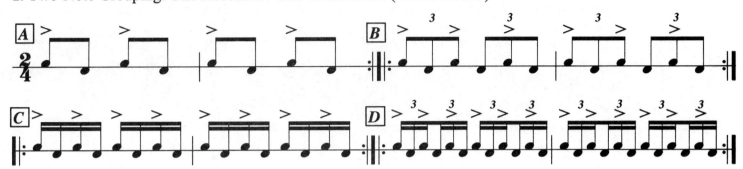

2. Two-Note Grouping: One Accented / One Unaccented (1st Inversion)

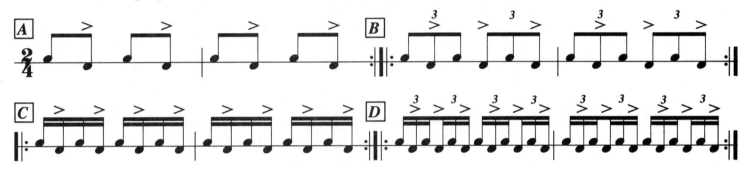

3. Three-Note Grouping: One Accented / Two Unaccented (Root Position)

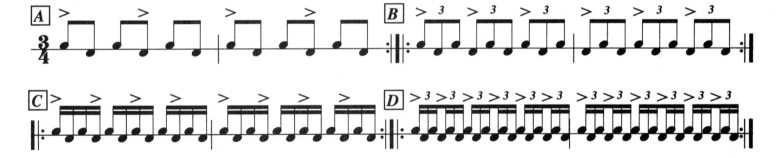

4. Three-Note Grouping: One Accented / Two Unaccented (1st Inversion)

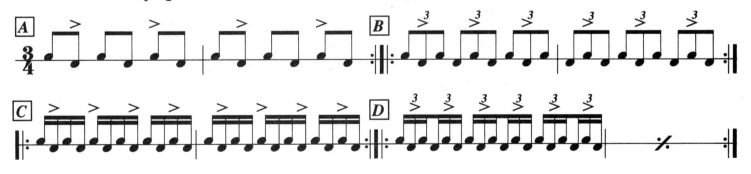

5. Three-Note Grouping: One Accented / Two Unaccented (2nd Inversion)

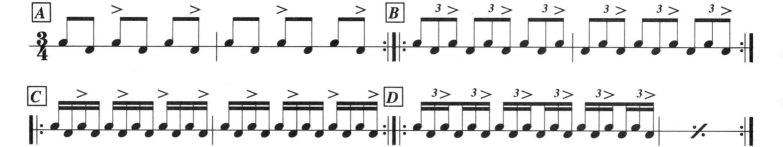

6. Three-Note Grouping: Two Accented / One Unaccented (Root Position)

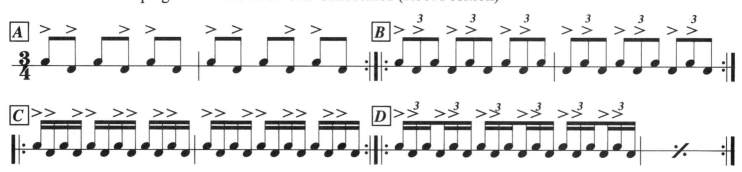

7. Three-Note Grouping: Two Accented / One Unaccented (1st Inversion)

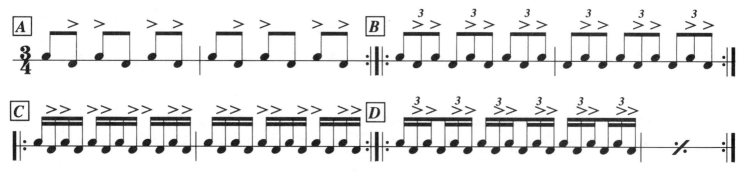

8. Three-Note Grouping: Two Accented / One Unaccented (2nd Inversion)

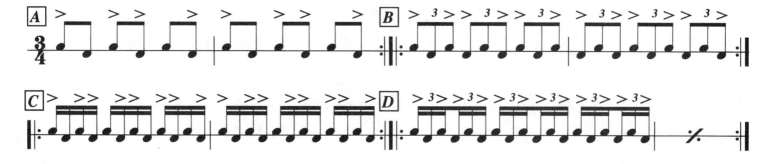

9. Four-Note Grouping: One Accented / Three Unaccented (Root Position)

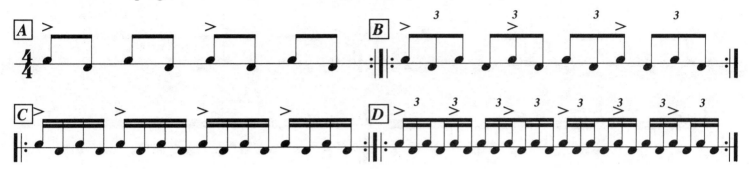

10. Four-Note Grouping: One Accented / Three Unaccented (1st Inversion)

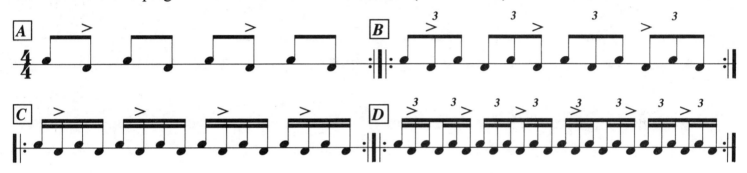

11. Four-Note Grouping: One Accented / Three Unaccented (2nd Inversion)

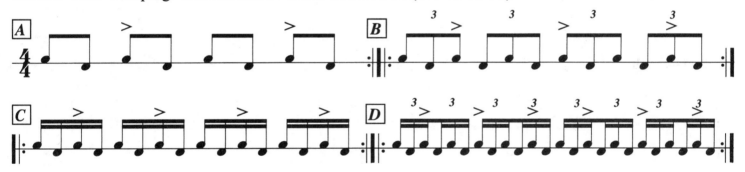

12. Four-Note Grouping: One Accented / Three Unaccented (3rd Inversion)

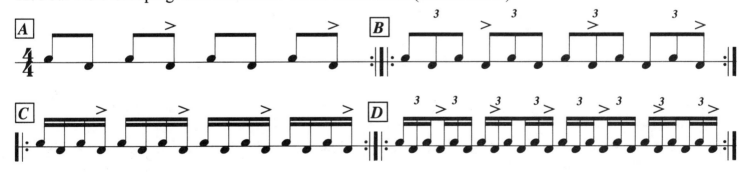

13. Four-Note Grouping: Two Accented / Two Unaccented (Root Position)

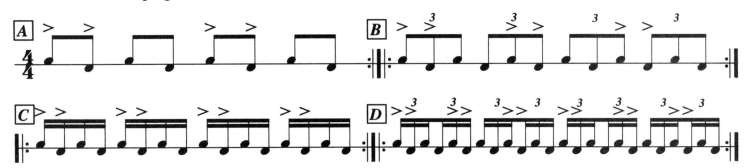

14. Four-Note Grouping: Two Accented / Two Unaccented (1st Inversion)

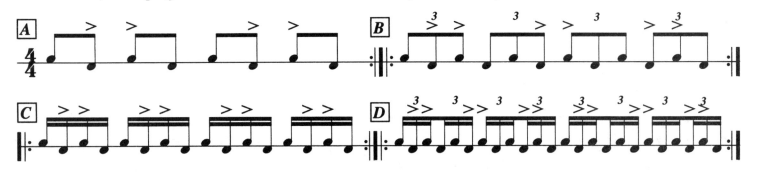

15. Four-Note Grouping: Two Accented / Two Unaccented (2nd Inversion)

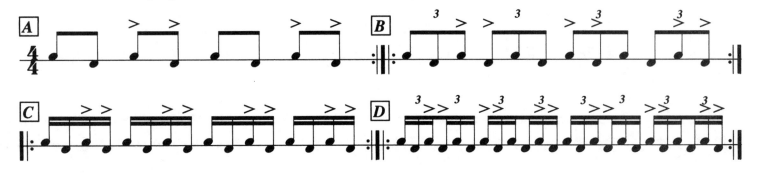

16. Four-Note Grouping: Two Accented / Two Unaccented (3rd Inversion)

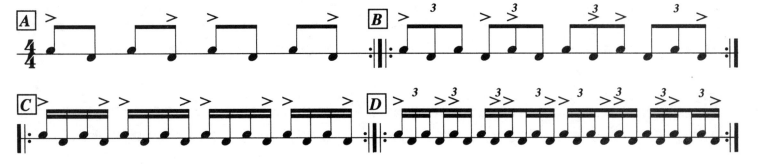

Accent Studies ~ Part IB: Selected Common Rhythmic Motives

1. 2/4 I

2. 2/4 II

3. 3/4 I

4. 3/4 II

5. 3/4 III

6. 4/4 I

7. 4/4 II

8. 4/4 III

9. 5/4 I

10. 5/4 II

11. 6/4

12. 7/4

If rhythm is considered the heartbeat of music then dynamics are its breathing lungs, continuously inhaling and exhaling to provide mood and emotion to its life. Without dynamics, music becomes a tiring wall of sound, or monotonous drone, with no color, drama, or offer of engagement to its listener. Think of how we speak. We not only use *rhythm* in the cadences of our speech we also employ *pitch* for intimation and *dynamics* for emphasis. As drummers we're expected to be able to shout, but it is important to also be able to whisper on our instrument, and command the range in between the extremes, all the while keeping up the drive and intensity. Music, like speech, is nothing more than waves of sound at its most fundamental level. Melody, harmony and rhythm are all the same thing, moving at different rates of speed. Dynamic control offers great challenges to drummers because it taps into balancing the relationships of the ever-changing velocities of tempo and volume. It also offers possibilities for better-attuned harmonic sensibilities.

Application

Keeping time steady when increasing or decreasing in volume is a common problem among musicians. As volume escalates be mindful of tempo. As the energy goes up so, inadvertently, can the pulse. Loud volume and *intensity* are often confused in music as being one and the same. They do often work hand in hand, but intensity of *tempo* must be maintained *throughout* the dynamic spectrum. Being mindful of tempo as the volume comes down is also important, so as not to drag the pulse. The studies on the following pages focus on effectively overcoming this dilemma.

Parts IA and IB apply a variety of *crescendo* and *diminuendo* sequences to the *Standard Timetable* (see the *Glossary of Terms*, pg. 135, for definitions of all terms and markings used in this chapter). Part IC applies a *measured* use of the full spectrum of dynamics (with *no* crescendo or diminuendo) to the increasing and decreasing subdivisions of the timetable in *Roundtable Form*. The *Etudes* in Part ID combine all the devices discussed.

Melodic and *harmonic* interpretations apply easily to the dynamic examples. Create pitch-bending effects by playing examples in Part IB with one hand, while applying and releasing pressure to the drumhead with your stick, hand, or elbow in the other. Visualize the *hairpin* marking, outlining crescendo and diminuendo (<), as being *high-pitched* (*with* pressure) on the *closed* end, and *low-pitched* (*no* pressure) on the *open* end. Part IE combines measured dynamics with intervals of common chord changes. Percussion raises *higher* in pitch when struck *louder* than it is when struck softer. Using your ear, employ *relative* pitch to assign the *piano* (*p*) dynamic as *tonic* and find the *root* intervals of the "chord changes" using the suggested dynamics as a *guide*. This only scratches the surface of applying melody and harmony to the drums in any key you're playing in. Check it out!

Practice Tips

The dynamic concepts presented in this chapter apply to *all* of the timetables in this book.

Crescendo & Diminuendo in Roundtable Form

1. Soft/Loud/Soft I

2. Loud/Soft/Loud I

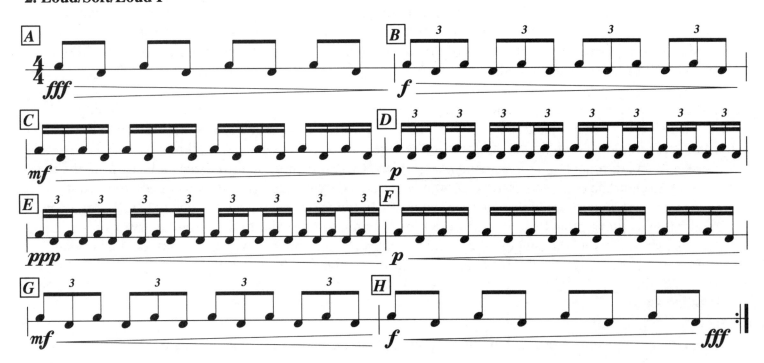

Crescendo & Diminuendo (or Pitch Bending Interpretation)

1. Soft/Loud/Soft II

2. Loud/Soft/Loud II

3. Soft to Loud (Repeating)

4. Loud to Soft (Repeating)

Measured Dynamic Changes in Roundtable Form

1. Soft/Loud/Soft III

Dynamic Control Etudes in Roundtable Form

1. Etude I

Measured Dynamic Changes Relative to Common Chord Change Intervals

1. p-mf-f-p/I-IV-V-I

2. p-ff-mp-f/I-vi-ii-V

3. mp-f-p/ ii-V-I

17

Interpretation Notes for Song Form Applications

The drumset is considered an instrument of indeterminate pitch, meaning it is typically not tuned like an instrument of determinate pitch (such as a piano). Therefore we must sometimes work harder to communicate with the average listener, who may not have a highly attuned ear for the nuances of the drum beyond an undeniable groove. This is where the architecture a song form provides becomes a useful tool. Structure gives context to our musical ideas. By employing musical devices such as *motives* (short rhythmic or melodic phrases), *themes* (combining a few short motives), *contrast* (introducing a new melodic, harmonic, rhythmic or dynamic element), and *sequencing* (transposing a motif into another register), to name a few, we create a musical vocabulary which we must then organize logically through the structure of form to intrigue our audience and capture their attention. The greatest improvisers in music can do this on the spot with the knowledge and experience they've acquired.

Application

We can incorporate forms beyond the recommended *Roundtable Form* to variations of the *Standard Timetable* to enhance our overall musical awareness while honing our timekeeping skills in the process. The short examples on the following page illustrate variations of four common musical forms. We will combine them with excerpts of examples previously seen in the *Standard Timetable in Roundtable Form*, *Accent Studies* and *Dynamic Control Studies* sections of the book.

The first two incorporate *antiphony*–the musical term for what is more commonly referred to as *call* and *response*, or *question* and *answer* form. Example 1 outlines a simple *Binary* form using two motives (A and B) that alternate in a question and answer fashion. As it is when teaching a child to speak or read, the use of repetition breeds familiarity with our phrasing for the listener. The Binary form is excellent for creating such a continuum. Example 2 is a shortened *Rondo* form variation, which establishes a call and response pattern where the call remains the same but the responses will be different–similar to a roll call vote in government. The Binary and Rondo forms can be employed quite effectively for long periods of time over a vamp or open solo.

Example 3 uses the common *AABA* form, typically 32 bars long, condensed here into four bars. Think of a presentation where you explain an idea (A). Repeat it for emphasis (A). Ask if there are questions (B–a contrast), and then sum up with a review of your idea (A).

Example 4 outlines an *8 Bar Blues* form variation, once again showing the chord changes and offering measured dynamic markings for exploring the relative pitches of the roots of the chords on the drums, as outlined in the previous section of the book.

Practice Tips

Apply any timetable in the book to these and as many other common song form variations as you can.

Musical Phrasing ~ Interpretation Notes for Song Form Applications

1. Binary Form (AB)

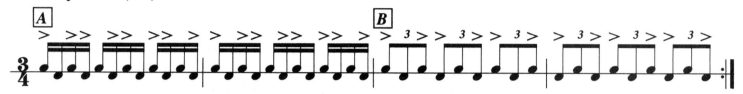

2. Rondo Form Variation (ABACAD)

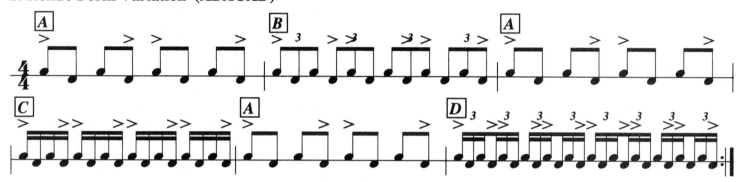

3. AABA Form Variation

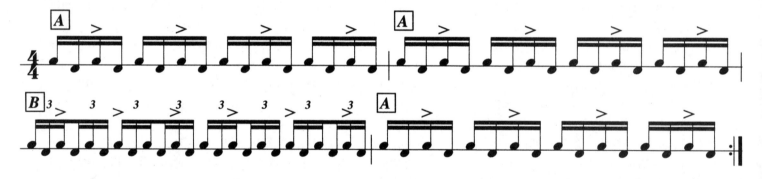

4. 8 Bar Blues: I-IV-I-VI-ii-V-I-V

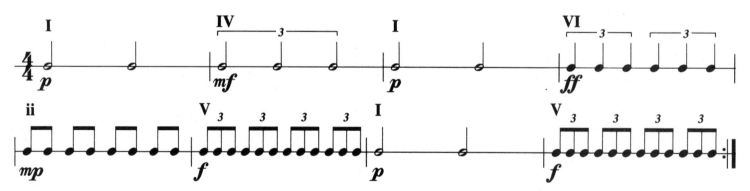

From the time we are born–learning to crawl, walk, run, and climb–coordination is an instinctual and natural function of our body. To develop coordination on the multiple percussion set-up that is the drumset, we must think of it in the collective sense, like our body, as one instrument. Any voice of the drumset can be played in isolation but as with the eighty-eight keys on a piano, how we combine the many voices into one is the artistic endeavor we pursue for greater musicality.

Application

Coordination is a tool for developing the freedom to spontaneously play what you hear in your head, staying focused on musical expression and not physical mechanics, when performing. On the following pages, the groupings in Part IA employ *harmonic coordination* (two or more voices played simultaneously). These examples focus on building a strong foundation of coordination in any combination of one, two, three or four limbs. Examples 1 and 2 apply alternating single strokes to *dependent coordination*, first by alternating both hands with both feet, and next by alternating the right limbs and left limbs. Examples 3 and 4 employ *independent coordination*, first by alternating single strokes in *contrary motion* (with one direction in the hands and another in the feet) and next layering single strokes in the hands over *double strokes* between the feet. Try also *switching* this combination, placing the doubles in the hands and singles in the feet. Play all of the examples isolating the sticking for each hand or foot. Reverse the stickings to help develop ambidexterity.

Examples 5 and 6 focus on being able to hear and control more than one rhythm at a time by establishing a drone in first the right then left *hand* (Ex. 5) and adding and subtracting combinations of the remaining three limbs in unison with it. Example 6 establishes the drone in first the right then left *foot* and builds from there in the same fashion. Strive for clean, unison phrasing in *all* of the above exercises, avoiding any "flamming."

Part IB explores *melodic coordination* (linear phrasing with only one hand or foot played at a time). These examples alternate one, two, three, and four note motives, respectively, between the hands and feet with a "fugue-like" approach to the phrasing as one voice (the feet) *imitates* another (the hands) in another register. Alternate stickings between the hands and feet are used in each example, with *mirrored sticking* options also illustrated for the *one* and *three* note motives. These examples are excellent for double bass drum applications but are also important to play with the HH as well for a different sound.

Practice Tips

The noteheads in the following examples can be interpreted as any voice on the drumset. Play the examples slowly, at first, and spiritedly. Use dynamics and experiment with tone. Continue coordination variations using these single-stroke roll sticking interpretations: RH/RF; LH/LF; RH/LF; LH/RF; BH/RF; BH/LF; RH/BF, and LH/BF.

4-Way Coordination Part IA: Harmonic Coordination Studies

1. Dependent Coordination (between Hands & Feet)

2. Dependent Coordination (between R & L Limbs)

3. Independent Coordination (between R & L Limbs)

4. Independent Coordination (between Hands & Feet)

5. Layered Unison Coordination I: Hands to Feet to Hands

6. Layered Unison Coordination II: Feet to Hands to Feet

4-Way Coordination Part IB: Melodic Coordination Studies

1. One Note (Mirroring between Hands & Feet)

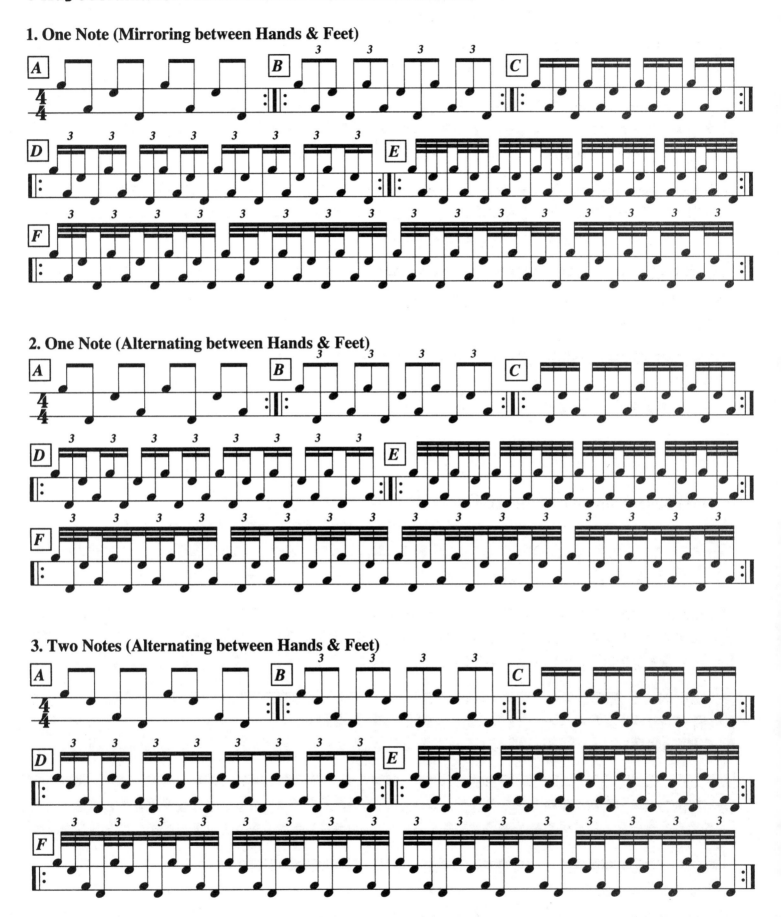

2. One Note (Alternating between Hands & Feet)

3. Two Notes (Alternating between Hands & Feet)

4. Three Notes (Mirroring between Hands & Feet)

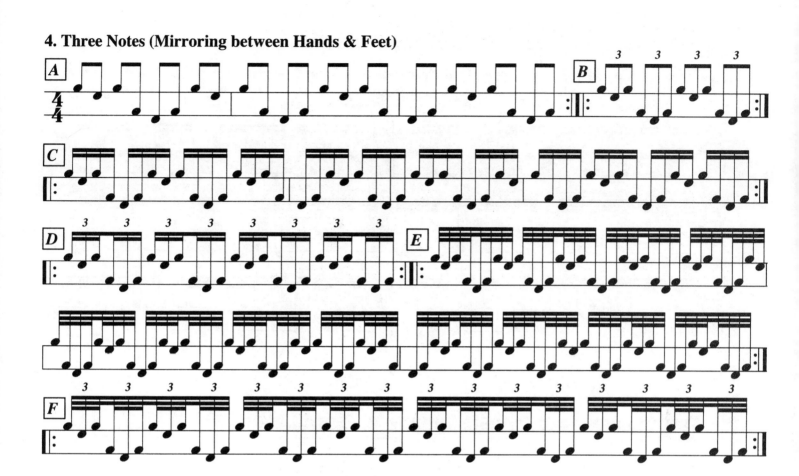

5. Three Notes (Alternating between Hands & Feet)

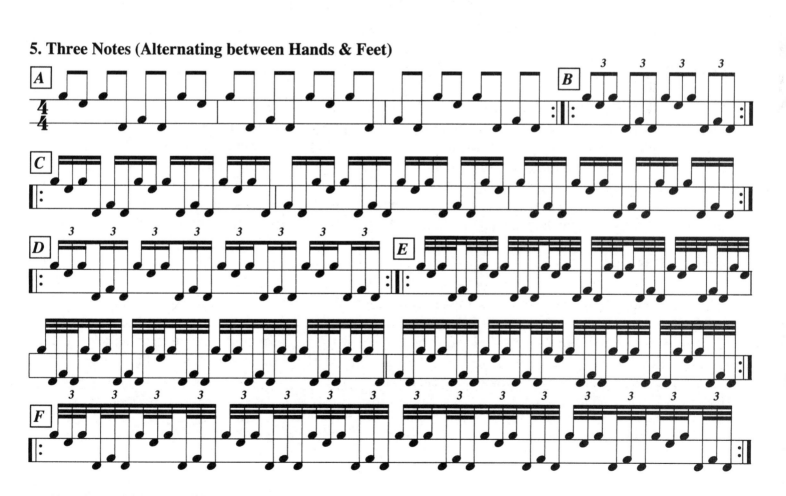

6. Four Notes (Alternating between Hands & Feet)

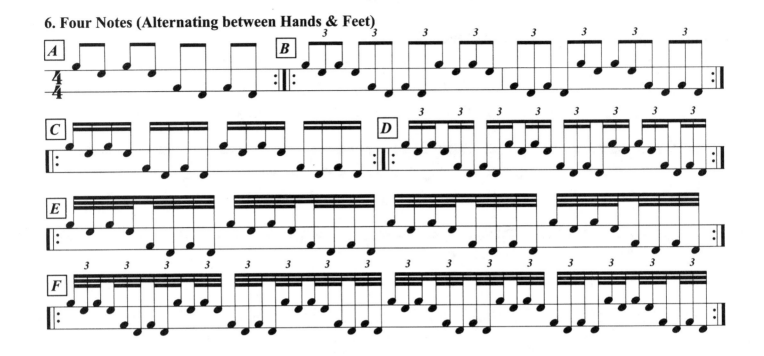

Chapter 2 ~ 4-Way Coordination
Part Two: Counterpoint Ostinato Options for Feet & Hands

Ostinatos are consistently repeating motives, usually in the same voice or voices. On the drumset, ostinatos are typically executed with one or more limbs to provide a rhythmic counterpoint for the remaining limbs to improvise over. This approach opens up the full potential for applying coordination to orchestration on the instrument.

Application

The ostinato examples for the feet and hands illustrated on the following pages are isolated from each other so that you can orchestrate any combination of rhythms you choose. The intent here is not to present an exhaustive collection of ostinatos, only a practical one. There are a limited number of rhythms but an infinite number of combinations. Any 8th or 16th note rhythms can be phrased with a swung feel when applied either throughout any timetable or just to its triplet subdivisions. Observe notes in parenthesis that can be omitted to create more rhythmic possibilities. Ostinatos illustrated with alternate stickings can be played with one limb and vice versa. Interpret these examples freely!

Practice Tips

These ostinatos can be applied to any timetable, in any time signature, presented in the book. Accompany timetables in 5/4, 6/4, or 7/4, by combining the 2/4, 3/4, or 4/4 ostinatos as, for example, 3/4+2/4 = 5/4; 3/4+3/4 or 2/4+2/4+2/4 = 6/4; and 4/4+3/4 = 7/4. Interpret your choices creatively by adding colors–like alternating open and closed tones with the HH foot–to any ostinato, or adding suitable accents to snare drum or cymbals, and so forth.

Counterpoint Ostinato Options for Feet

I. Bass Drum(s)

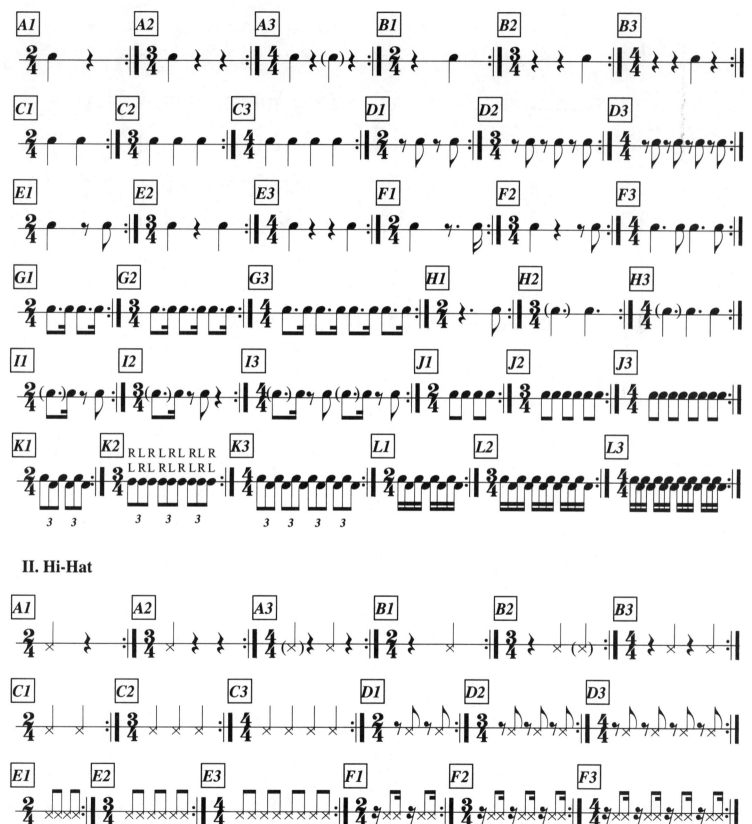

II. Hi-Hat

Counterpoint Ostinato Options for Hands

I. Ride Cymbal / Hi-Hat / Other

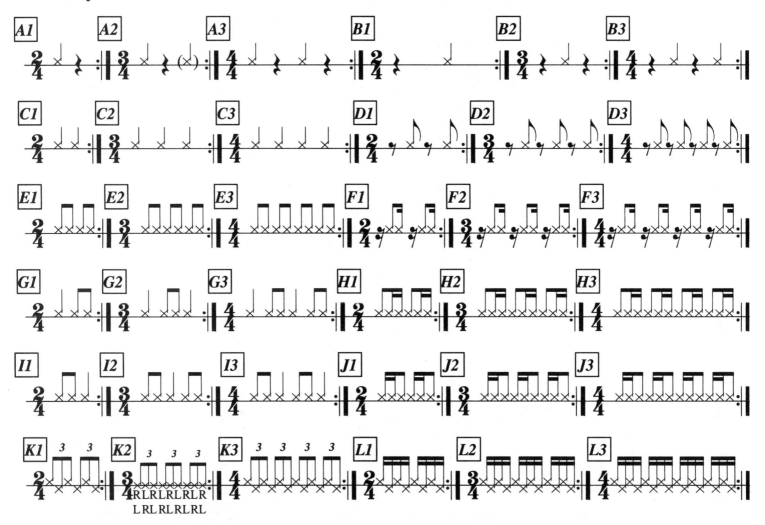

II. Snare Drum / Cross-stick

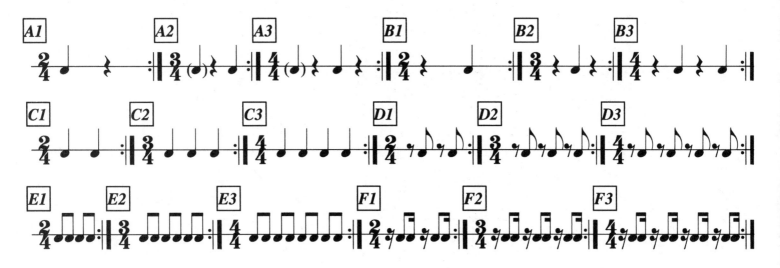

Part One: Long Roll Studies

Rudimental stickings were originally designed to give the snare drummer a rhythmic vocabulary with which to build a foundation for executing military cadences with consistent precision and a bit of flair as well. Their incorporation into classical and jazz music elevated rudimental drumming to a greater art form that continues today in many styles of music. The true foundations of all rudiments are the long roll variations. A long roll is a continuous repetition of strokes, creating a drone, typically lasting over one or more bars of music. The standard combinations, illustrated on the following pages, are the single-stroke, buzz-stroke, double-stroke and triple-stroke rolls.

Application

Begin by working through each variation at a tempo where you can easily execute all of the subdivisions. Don't be concerned with speed as much as with developing relaxed, even strokes for each variation. As you begin to flow with greater ease through the subdivisions, you can increase the tempo gradually. Avoid accents, at first, in your execution but do apply a variety of dynamic levels to the variations for greater control.

"What type of roll do I use and when?" is a common musical question more easily answered if you understand the sound textures each variation provides. *Single strokes* give you, first and foremost, power. When needed, nothing is stronger than a single blow followed by another from the opposite arm. They are the best strokes for achieving a purely staccato articulation at any dynamic level. *Buzz strokes*, by contrast, are designed to provide a smoother continuum of sound with a lighter, more legato articulation. Somewhere in between are the *double* and *triple strokes* - providing a more staccato attack when played in a more open fashion and suggesting a more legato flow when played in a more closed one. Many rhythmic phrases can be played with any of the common long roll stickings. Let tempo, dynamics, taste and imagination be your guides.

Practice Tips

Play the examples as written and with the stickings reversed. Interpret them (excepting buzz strokes) substituting your feet for your hands. Choose accompaniment for these variations from the *Counterpoint Ostinato Options* on pg.25. Coordination can be further advanced by substituting one or both feet for either hand, combining limbs in the patterns. Applying a variety of wrist control, finger control or open/close hand techniques and heel down, heel up, rocking, or swivel foot techniques to the variations can advance your technique greatly. Swing the duple subdivisions in the exercises to add dimension to the feel. Add accents from *Musical Phrasing Part I* (pg. 3) to *all* of the roll variations.

Experiment with tonal color by practicing the examples with sticks, brushes, mallets and hands as well as combinations of these. Apply the stickings around the drumset to create musical motives and phrases.

1. Single-Stroke Roll

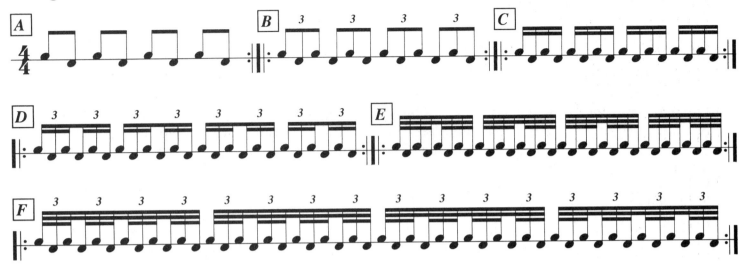

2. Buzz-Stroke Roll

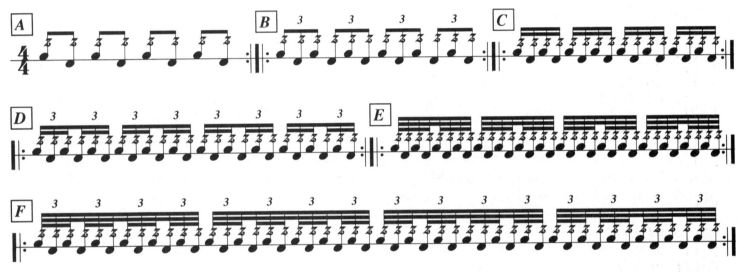

3. Double-Stroke Roll

4. Inverted Double-Stroke Roll

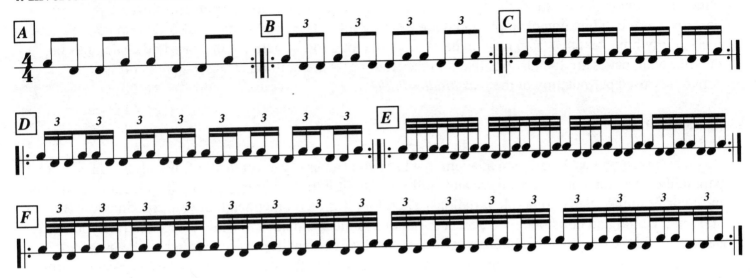

5. Triple-Stroke Roll

Paradiddle stickings are extremely versatile rudimental variations. They are perhaps most simply described as a combination of single and double stroke rolls. The combinations also contain very musical rhythmic textures from hand to hand. Like the long roll variations, the paradiddle stickings on the following pages are foundations that all other rudiments are built on. The *six-stroke roll* is a commonly used permutation of the *paradiddle-diddle*.

Application

Begin by practicing each variation at a tempo where you can easily execute all of the subdivisions. Each paradiddle variation contains a unique and earthy *feel* built into its sticking–giving it an identity different in flavor from the related long roll variations. Therefore it is recommended that you experiment with applying natural and other common accent variations to these timetables, while also spreading your hands around the drumset, to explore a variety of tonal variations for groove, ensemble phrasing and soloing motives. Try superimposing the *two* and *four-note* accent groupings from *Musical Phrasing Part I* (pg. 3) over the *single* and *triple paradiddle* stickings and the *three-note* accent groupings over the *double paradiddle* and *paradiddle-diddle* stickings. Note also the illustrated accents common to the six-stroke roll.

With the paradiddle-diddle rudiment, permutations are included that, by *inversion*, illustrate common examples of a measured six-stroke roll (see *Glossary of Terms*, pg. 135). Timetables focusing on other measured five, seven and nine-stroke rolls will be examined in *Volume II*. Although not illustrated in this text, the common sticking inversions of the single paradiddle (LRRL-RLLR, RRLR-LLRL, and RLRL-LRLR) are excellent studies for timetable application as well. It is worth noting that the same goes for inversions of the triple-stroke roll (RLL-LRR and LLR-RRL) on pg. 30.

Remember to practice all examples with the written and reversed stickings. Also note the variations between the subdivisions used in the paradiddle-diddle timetable and the six-stroke roll inversion timetables. This was done in the interest of conserving space. The important thing to realize as you encounter these variations is that *any Standard Timetable* in the text can be applied to *any* subdivision grouping illustrated in the *Standard Timetable Presented in Roundtable Form* on pg. 2.

Practice Tips

As with previous studies, incorporating the feet by substituting one or both feet for either hand and even doubling the hands when doing so, or incorporating accompaniment from the *Counterpoint Ostinato Options* on pg. 25, are all excellent methods for creating colorful grooves and solo motives. Swinging the duple subdivisions and/or substituting flams, drags or buzz strokes for accented notes in the above-suggested manner also offers *great* dimension to the musical possibilities.

1. Single Paradiddle

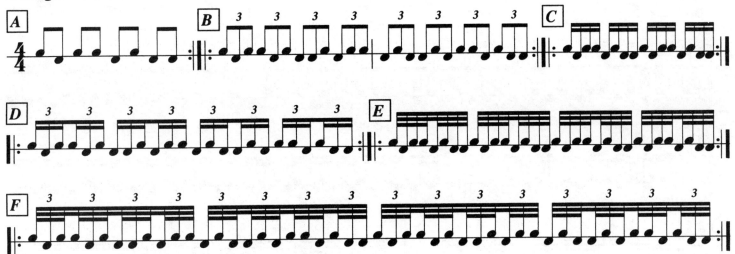

2. Double Paradiddle

3. Triple Paradiddle

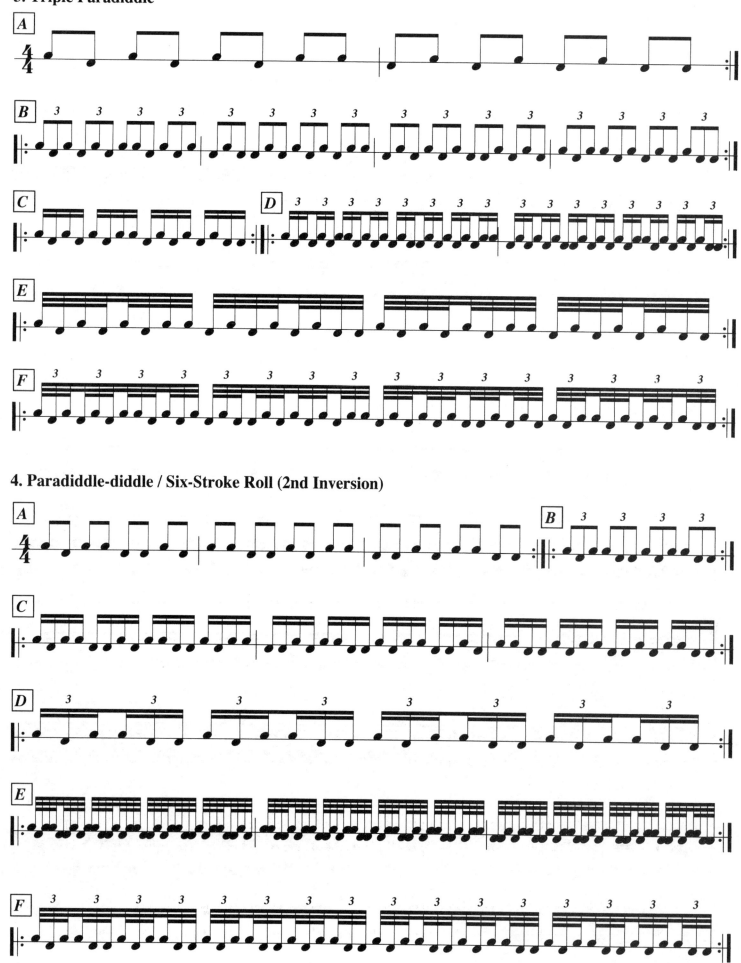

4. Paradiddle-diddle / Six-Stroke Roll (2nd Inversion)

5. Six-Stroke Roll (Root Position)

6. Six-Stroke Roll (1st Inversion)

7. Six-Stroke Roll (3rd Inversion)

Flam rudiments typically embellish foundational long or measured rolls and paradiddle variations as outlined in *Selected Rudimental Variations Parts One* and *Two*. Flams are traditionally executed by playing a grace note with one hand just ahead of a primary note fitting into a particular rhythmic subdivision with the other. Flams can enhance phrasing both by providing a natural accent (due to the offset execution of the grace and primary notes) and by adding a rhythmic counterpoint to the foundational rudiment in use.

Application

The examples on the following pages outline the above concept. The *pataflafla* and *flam accents* apply rhythmic flam counterpoint to a *single-stroke roll* foundation. The *Swiss windmill* does the same over an *inverted single paradiddle* sticking (RRLR-LLRL). And the *alternating flams, flam tap, tap flam,* and *Swiss triplets* are all based on the *double-stroke roll* as follows: The flam tap and tap flam add counterpoint to double-stroke and inverted double-stroke roll foundations; the alternating flams and Swiss triplets *are*, in fact, *obscured* double-stroke rolls themselves. In the case of the alternating flams the *doubled note* in each hand lands closer than usual to the down stroke in the opposite hand, and in the case of the Swiss triplets the double strokes *overlap* each other.

Understanding these relationships provides perspective to incorporate flams creatively and effectively in musical application. To develop your control, use your imagination to integrate the following flam rudiment timetables with their foundational ones in *Selected Rudimental Variations Parts One* and *Two* (pgs. 28-34).

Practice Tips

Traditionally flams are executed with the *grace note* landing from a *low* stick height, for a *softer* sound, and the *primary note* from a *higher* height, for a *louder* one. Once you've mastered this approach, experiment with reversing those dynamics or playing the grace and primary strokes at equal volumes. It is also interesting to experiment with the *space* between the grace and primary strokes. Try widening them enough to produce a "shuffled" rhythm then gradually tightening them all the way into a perfect unison, also known as a "flat flam." Note that all of the examples in this section are notated in the traditional manner except the Swiss triplet variations, which are written as "flat flams" since it is a common application of this rudiment as voiced around the drumset. Apply extremes in widening or tightening the flams to any of the following exercises.

Playing the examples accompanied by selections from the *Counterpoint Ostinato Options for Feet* on pg. 26, is recommended for both the written and reversed stickings. Also try using call and response form by alternating the execution of each subdivision with first the hands and then the feet. Try playing just the grace notes with your feet, or the reverse, and voicing the hands around the drumset.

1. Alternating Flams

2. Flam Tap

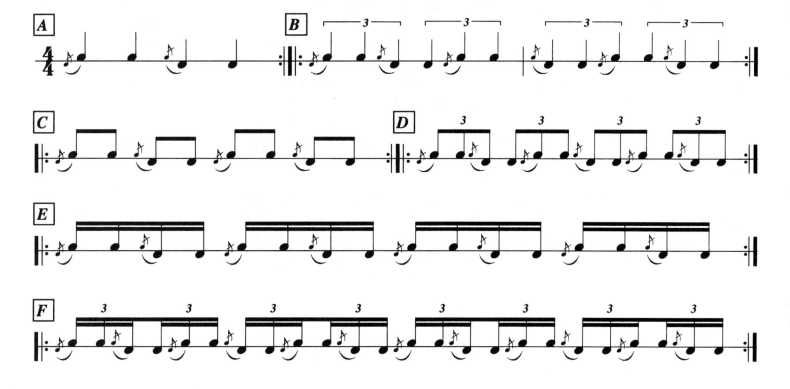

3. Tap Flam

4. Pataflafla

5. Swiss Windmill

6. Flam Accent (Root Position)

7. Flam Accent (1st Inversion)

8. Flam Accent (2nd Inversion)

9. Swiss Triplet (Root Position)

10. Swiss Triplet (1st Inversion)

11. Swiss Triplet (2nd Inversion)

Drag rudiments, like the flam ones, also add embellishment to rudimental long or measured rolls and paradiddle variations. As flams are a two-note combination, executed with a grace note in one hand just ahead of a primary note in the other, drags are a three-note combination executed by playing two grace notes with one hand ahead of a primary note with the other. Drags enhance phrasing by providing a rolling, rhythmic continuum of varying degrees within the foundational stickings they are applied to.

Application

As with flams, drags offer phrasing flexibility in the *space* between the grace and primary strokes. The double-stroked *grace notes* of the drag are typically interpreted in any one of *three* different rhythmic subdivisions. Thinking of a *quarter-note* on the *downbeat* as our *primary* stroke, doubling the *sixteenth-note* just before it would produce an example of a *closed drag*. Doubling the *eighth-note* ahead of the downbeat would produce a *half-open drag*. Playing the second and third partials of an *eighth-note triplet* ahead of the downbeat produces a *fully-open drag*. A succession of fully-open drags would sound like evenly subdivided eighth-note triplets, traditionally executed with the *grace notes* played *softer* dynamically, and the *primary note* being *accented*.

The examples on the following pages are based on the *fully-open drag* interpretation. Letter B in the first timetable (*Open Drag w/RH Lead*) is the rhythmic foundation for the whole series. The grace and primary notes of the drag flow at the same rate of speed in all of the duple and triple rhythms, compressing as the subdivisions increase and expanding as they decrease. Example 7 (the "Egg Beater") is a variation of the example 6 inversion, superimposing a *triple-stroke* over the *doubled* grace note and a *double-stroke* over the primary, *single accented note*. Here the basic count is included for each subdivision.

Variations on the open drag are presented in both 3/4 and 4/4 time signatures, to demonstrate both basic and "over-the-bar" phrasing. The open drag is illustrated in *root position* and *inversion* sequencing (see *Glossary of Terms*, pg. 135) to illuminate further phrasing options that are available and commonly used with this rudiment. Note that the sticking is inconsistent in the inversion sequence, flipping from right-hand to left-hand lead. This is purposeful to accentuate common applications. Always remember it is recommended to practice *all* examples with written and reversed stickings.

Practice Tips

Play the examples on the snare drum (with sticks, brushes, etc.) then experiment with spreading your hands around the drumset. Play with RH on ride cymbal, HH, or cowbell and LH on snare drum (adding the BD tastefully in unison with the RH) for linear groove applications. Try swinging the duple subdivisions and combining examples from the *Counterpoint Ostinato Options* on pg. 25, with the above ideas. You can play just the grace notes with your feet or hands, and even *split* the *doubled note* between two feet or hands, when playing the primary note with the opposite limb(s). Experiment!

1. Open Drag w/RH Lead (Root Position)

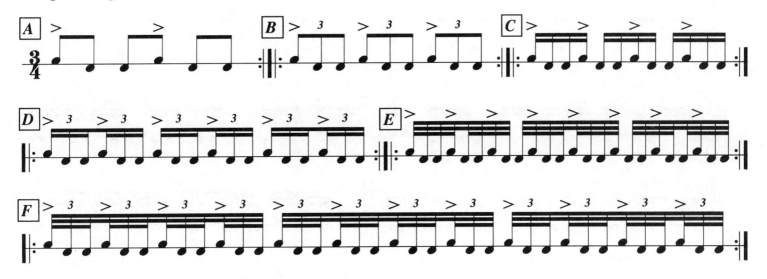

2. Open Drag w/LH Lead (1st Inversion)

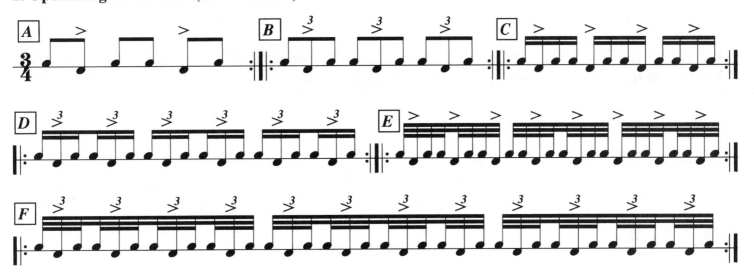

3. Open Drag w/LH Lead (2nd Inversion)

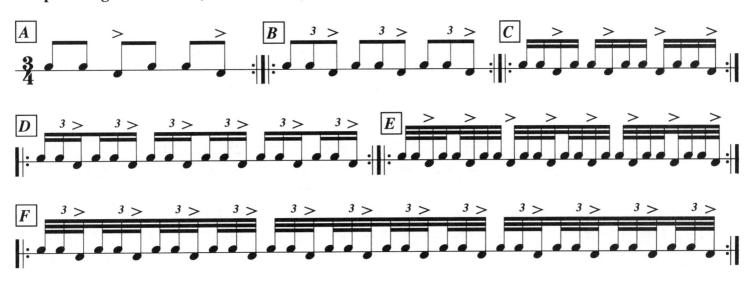

4. Open Drag w/RH Lead (Root Position)

5. Open Drag w/LH Lead (1st Inversion)

43

6. Open Drag w/LH Lead (2nd Inversion)

7. Open Drag w/LH Lead (2nd Inversion) - "Egg Beater" Variation

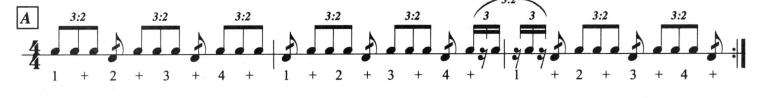

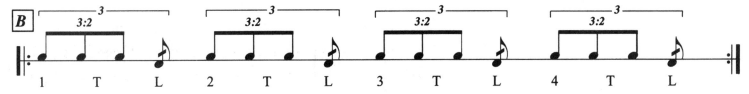

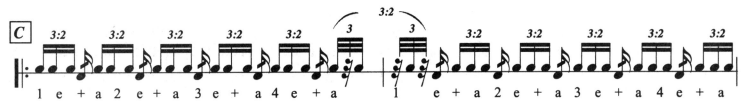

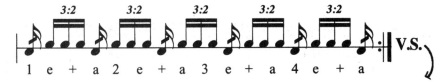

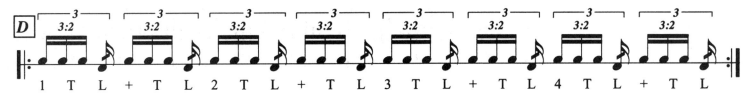

One virtue of the *Standard Timetable* as applied to the *Selected Rudimental Variations*, and other chapters of this book, is how it illustrates phrasing options for many rhythms beyond their conventional application. Imagination is the key to interpreting *all* of the examples of this text, but in order to do that it helps to have a sense of context. Flam and Drag rudiments, as previously mentioned, are similar in their usage as embellishments applied to rudimental long or measured rolls and paradiddle variations. So, just as we would want to know various scales to embellish melodically over a series of harmonic chord changes, it is useful to explore further ways flams and drags can embellish basic rudimental foundations and enhance our creative options rhythmically.

Application

The text for *Selected Rudimental Variations Part Three: Flam Studies*, pg. 35, outlines the connection of each flam rudiment in that section to its respective single, double-stroke and paradiddle sticking foundations. It is mentioned that the alternating flams and Swiss triplets are foundationally double stroke variations themselves. This perspective is based on their RR-LL stickings, which in the case of the alternating flams, *widen* the execution of the doubled note in each hand and, in the case of the Swiss triplets, *overlap* the double strokes in each hand. It is worth mentioning that, more commonly, *alternating flams* are interpreted as flams applied to a *single-stroke roll*. Many phrasing options spring from this perspective as well. Also note that the *Swiss triplet* can be interpreted as an ornamentation of the *open drag* by adding a flam to the first of the doubled notes of the sticking. Compare Letter D of example 9, *Swiss Triplet (Root Position)*, pg. 40, to Letter B of example 6, *Open Drag w/LH Lead (2nd Inversion)*, pg. 44, for an illustrated example. All of these options invite greater musical possibilities with experimentation. The "double-stroke" perspective offers greater ease in *executing* alternating flams and Swiss triplets, particularly at faster tempos.

Practice Tips

The following page offers a few more examples of flam and drag rudiments that can be applied to the single-stroke, double-stroke, inverted double-stroke, and single paradiddle timetables found in *Selected Rudimental Variations Part One: Long Roll Studies,* pg. 28. Each rudiment is presented in both duple and triple eighth-note forms, in time signatures relative to length of the phrase per subdivision. The stickings easily expand or compress into any note value grouping (i.e. *half, quarter, sixteenth,* or *thirty-second* notes) used in the timetables and can be applied to any time signature. Note that the *drags* in these examples are interpreted *half-open*, doubling any related single stroke, to keep the flow steady per subdivision. Apply flams or half-open drags *before, on,* and *after* the accented notes throughout *Musical Phrasing Part One: Accents Studies,* pg. 3, for more phrasing options. Finally, keep in mind you are not *limited* to "rudimental foundations" when using flams and drags. Experiment!

Interpretation Notes for Further Flam and Drag Studies

Single-Stroke Roll Variations

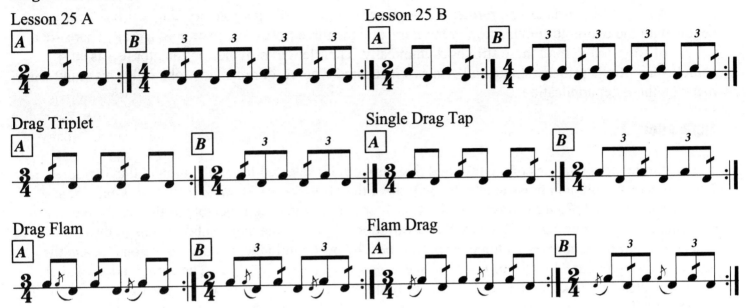

Double-Stroke and Inverted Double-Stroke Roll Variations

Single Paradiddle Variations

Four and five-stroke ruffs extend further the sequence of embellishing a primary single stroke that begins with the two-note combination of the flam, and the three-note combination of a drag. There are a variety of ways to interpret these strokes rhythmically. Their length provides options for use as an embellishment of a primary stroke and also as a measured type of four or five-stroke roll. This study will focus on the latter application.

Application

The rhythmic interpretations of the four and five-stroke ruffs selected for application to the *Standard Timetable* are common in musical phrasing. Observe the *Four-Stroke Ruff (Root Position)*, pg. 48, and the *Five-Stroke Ruff (Root Position)*, pg. 49. Consider Letter D in each timetable as the "root rhythm" (see *Glossary of Terms*. pg. 135) for each ruff variation. Note that the *triple* subdivisions in these timetables *retain* the motives within their pulses, beat by beat, while the *duple* subdivisions *spread* the motives "over-the-bar," by way of *hemiola* (see *Glossary of Terms*, pg. 135). The combination of short and long notes that make up the ruffs offers our first look at an *abstraction* of the flow of subdivisions in the *Standard Timetable*. Here, instead of an *even* or *steady* flow of notes, compressing or expanding around the quarter-note pulse, we have an *uneven* or *broken* flow of notes occurring within the subdivisions of the timetable. More examples of this kind are illustrated and explained in *Chapter 4 ~ Abstract Timetable Studies* (see pg. 51).

Note that the rhythms in this section have been neutralized on the staff line to allow for a variety of sticking applications. As embellishments, the ruffs would typically be played with single strokes, but as measured rolls, or better still–*phrases*, the more stickings you can apply, the more possibilities you have–especially when voicing the rhythms around the drumset. Here are some sticking options, applicable to *all* subdivisions and inversions for both ruffs:

Four-Stroke Ruff	**Five-Stroke Ruff**
RLRL	RLRLR-LRLRL
RRLL	RRLLR-LLRRL
RLRR-LRLL	RLRRL
RRLR-LLRL	RRLRL

Practice Tips

Begin slowly. Increase tempo as you become comfortable with the sticking variations and overall feel of the rhythms. Play the examples on the snare drum then experiment with spreading your hands around the drumset. Add flams or try reversing the sticking variations. Reinterpret the stickings with all limbs, substituting either foot for either hand, etc. Play the examples with the RH on the ride or HH cymbals for timekeeping variations.

1. Four-Stroke Ruff (Root Position)

2. Four-Stroke Ruff (1st Inversion)

3. Four-Stroke Ruff (2nd Inversion)

4. Five-Stroke Ruff (Root Position)

5. Five-Stroke Ruff (1st Inversion)

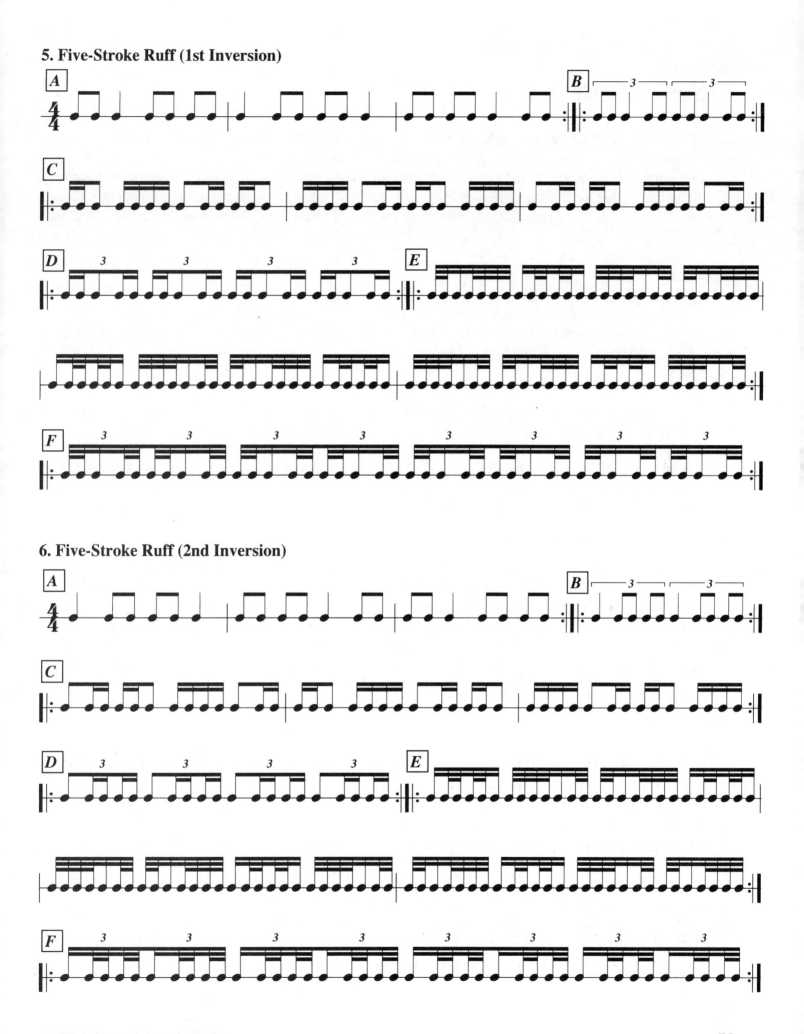

6. Five-Stroke Ruff (2nd Inversion)

Chapter 4
Abstract Timetable Studies

The following pages illustrate examples of what are referred to in this text as *Abstract Timetables* (see *Glossary of Terms*, pg. 135). The concept of the *Abstract Timetable* allows for the exploration of rhythmic phrases that vary from the common flow of subdivisions of the *Standard Timetable*, but are effectively applicable to the timetable format. Two particular applications of the *Abstract Timetable* are introduced on the following pages and a variety are employed throughout the text and typically noted as such.

Application

The examples on pg. 52 introduce the *Syncopated Standard Timetable*. Syncopation (see *Glossary of Terms*, pg. 135), shifts accents from *strong* beats (like downbeats) to normally *weak* ones (like upbeats). We incorporate syncopation into the *Standard Timetable* by displacing (*shifting*) its common subdivisions.

Displacing the note value groupings of the *Standard Timetable Mainframe* to their respective *upbeats* (the 2nd partial of each note's value), *abstracts* them into a *syncopated* rhythm. The *Syncopated Standard Timetables in Duration* and *Attack Notation* illustrate this. The full note values in the *STT Mainframe* remain consistent in the *Syncopated STT in Duration Notation*. *The Syncopated STT in Attack Notation* focuses only on the rhythmic attack of the syncopated subdivisions–*not* their full duration. It will also be used in the *Contemporary Backbeat & Modern Jazz Groove Studies* chapters of the book.

The measured rudimental roll known as the *Single Stroke Four* offers a unique subdivision application to the *Standard Timetable* with its broken rhythmic flow and triplet-based foundation. The *Four-Stroke Roll* variations (pgs. 53 & 54) are illustrated in *root position* and its *inversions* (see *Glossary of Terms*, pg. 135), in both *Binary Phrasing* (a two beat pulse per subdivision), and *Dotted Motive Phrasing* (a three beat pulse per subdivision). All are common uses of this rudiment applying easily to the *Standard Timetable* through abstraction. *Ratamacue* and *Ratamaflam* rudimental variations are introduced in Examples 4 and 5 of the *Dotted Motive Phrasing* inversions, as embellishments of the *Four-Stroke Roll*.

Practice Tips

The *Attack Notation* timetable is an *excellent* foundation for advanced applications of 4/4 examples from the *Accent Studies* and *Rudimental Variations* sections of the book. Apply the stickings as you would to the *STT Mainframe*, but in the syncopated rhythm. Combine this with selected *Counterpoint Ostinato Options*, pg. 25. Try interpreting each note value of the *Duration Notation* example by inserting a two or three note subdivision that will fit *inside* of a larger note (as eighth or sixteenth subdivisions fit into a quarter-note, etc.). The smaller subdivision within creates *sustain*. *Accenting* each cycle distinguishes the phrasing of the *wider* subdivision. Try it with a half-open or fully-open drag. Any of the sticking variations discussed above can be interpreted mixing the feet with the hands and voicing all limbs around the drumset. Use your imagination. That's what abstract thinking is all about!

Abstract Timetable Studies: The Syncopated Standard Timetable

STT Mainframe

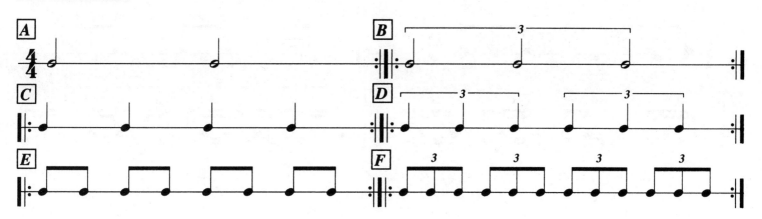

The Syncopated STT in Duration Notation

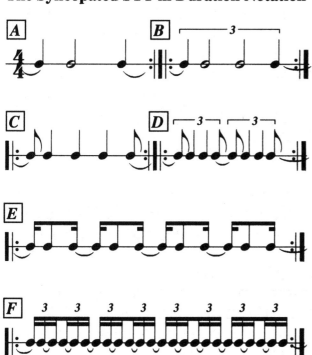

The Syncopated STT in Attack Notation

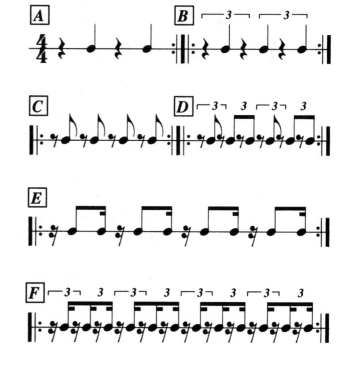

Abstract Timetable Studies: Variations on the Four-Stroke Roll

1. Four-Stroke Roll with Binary Phrasing

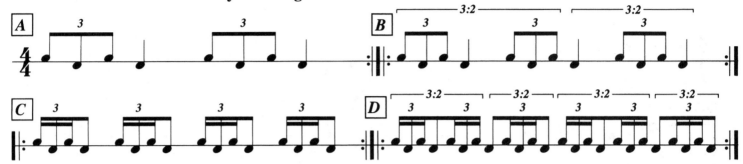

2. Inverted Four-Stroke Roll with Binary Phrasing

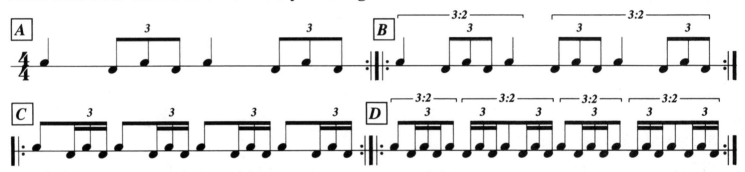

3. Four-Stroke Roll (Root Position) with Dotted Motive Phrasing

4. Four-Stroke Roll/Ratamacue Variation (1st Inversion) with Dotted Motive Phrasing

5. Four-Stroke Roll/Ratamaflam Variation (2nd Inversion) with Dotted Motive Phrasing

Polyrhythms and polyphony are musical reflections of the world in motion around us. "Poly" means many. As polyphony employs two or more harmonically related melodic voices speaking simultaneously, polyrhythms coordinate two or more rhythms– each with their own metrically divided duration–into a simultaneous cycle. Organized musical sound is a phenomenon adapted from nature. Melody, harmony, and rhythm are all one thing–pulsating waves of sound, simply moving at different rates of speed. Combining the same ratios of different frequencies vibrating simultaneously produces harmony and polyrhythm, respectively. The different frequencies of vibration produce a series of overtones that we hear as pitches when cycling faster and feel as rhythm when cycling slower. Hemiola is a rhythmic form of counterpoint that introduces a new type of meter on top of a previously existing one, creating a polyrhythm. Hemiola is to rhythm what a leading tone is to melody, and a suspended chord is to harmony–each engages the listener by creating an unexpected tension, if not quickly resolved.

Application

To build a strong foundation for exploring the "three-dimensional" aspect that a polyrhythm provides musically, it is necessary to master the fundamental primer examples on the following page. Examples 1 and 2 illustrate the duple and triple subdivision groupings of the *Standard Timetable*, isolated from each other. This isolation heightens the rhythmic tension or release from one subdivision to the next more so than when the duple and triple groupings are combined as a gradually compressing or expanding rhythmic scale. This concept applies also to Examples 3 & 4, which introduce new *Abstract Timetables*, isolating dotted subdivisions in 3/4 and 4/4 time. In these variations, Letter B, the *dotted* quarter-note pulse, is the "root rhythm" (see *Glossary of Terms*, pg. 135), that the related subdivisions "spring from." The dotted half-notes (Letter A) then flow *half* as fast, the dotted 8^{ths} (Letter C) flow *twice* as fast, and the dotted 16^{ths} (Letter D) flow *three times* as fast as Letter B.

With this foundation, we can explore linear, melodic and (in *Part Two* of this chapter) layered, harmonic phrasing studies. The *Hemiola Phrasing Progressions* (pg. 57) outline a Pan-African styled rhythmic alternative to the traditional method of using ritardando and accelerando for opening and closing a long roll. By combining duple, triple, dotted, and dotted-motive "shuffle" rhythms, phrased both "on-the-beat" and "over-the-bar," into a cycle that compresses or expands in *time* (depending on direction of flow*)*, wonderful phrasing options for both grooves and soloing are created. Note that minor gaps occur in the cycle. A few uncommon subdivisions have been purposely removed so as not to bog the organic flow of time down with confusing mathematics. The *Common Polyrhythmic Phrasing Progressions* (pg. 60) do not cross bar lines but are similar in concept. These progressions also draw their magic from how their motives compress or expand in whichever direction you flow from one subdivision to the next (*particularly* if you focus on interpreting the full value of each note for maximum effect).

Practice Tips

Separate the hands (and substitute either foot for either hand) around the drumset to create endless voicing options.

Polyrhythm Primer Isolating Subdivisions by Type

1. Isolating Duple Subdivisions

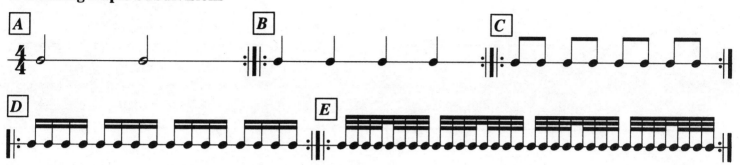

2. Isolating Triple Subdivisions

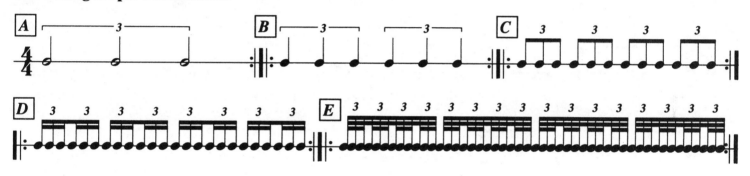

3. Isolating Dotted Subdivisions in 3/4

4. Isolating Dotted Subdivisions in 4/4

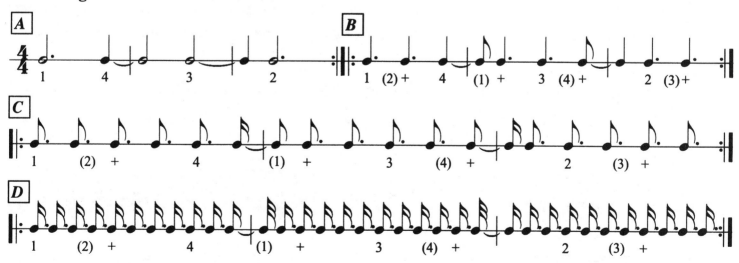

Hemiola Phrasing Progressions

1. Long Roll Progression I (Single Strokes)

2. Long Roll Progression IIA (Double Strokes)

3. Long Roll Progression IIB (Flam Tap Variation)

Common Polyrhythmic Phrasing Progressions

1. Root Position

2. 1st Inversion

3. 2nd Inversion

4. 3rd Inversion

The use of two or more metric frameworks played simultaneously–what we define as a polyrhythm–is the rhythmic foundation underlying African-influenced music worldwide. It is enlightening to understand the close connection between music and dance to tonal and telegraphic drum languages in the African culture. In many African languages the idea of a song, a rhythm, a dance, or even a drum, are not defined as separate entities but rather parts-of-the-whole of a single concept. This philosophy is useful for embracing the importance and inseparable relationship of drumming to dancing, to create a foundation for playing polyrhythms that allows any voice in a coordinated rhythm to lead or accompany in a clear, singing, and hard-grooving, danceable manner.

Application

To mathematically ascertain any polyrhythm, determine the meter of your foundation or "root rhythm," and the polymeter you would like to play over it. Apply a subdivision that equals the number of beats in the *polymeter* to each pulse of the "root rhythm" meter, and divide *that* subdivision by the number of beats in the "*root rhythm*." Execute by playing or accenting only those notes while keeping time in the original meter, and remember that the key to making the polyrhythms "sing and dance" lies outside the equation.

On the following page, consider Letter A of examples 1-3 as the "root rhythm" (see *Glossary of Terms*, pg. 135) for each polyrhythm. To determine *3:2 in 4/4*, step your feet on beats *1 and 3* of the quarter-note pulse, outlining the *"two-feel."* Count 8th note triplets, clapping the stressed beats: "**1**TL-**2**TL-**3**TL-**4**TL," to feel the three-over-two pulse. With *2:3 in 3/4*, step to the *quarter-note* pulse, outlining the *"three-feel."* Count 8th notes, clapping the stressed beats: "**1**&-**2**&-**3**&," to feel the two-over-three pulse. With *3:4 in 4/4*, step to the *quarter-note* pulse, outlining the *"four-feel."* Count 8th note triplets, again clapping the stressed beats: "**1**TL-**2**TL-**3**TL-**4**TL," to feel the three-over-four pulse. In these examples, the polyrhythms are simply played *twice* as fast at Letter B, *three* times as fast at Letter C, and *four* times as fast at Letter D. To determine *4:3 in 3/4*, consider Letter B the "root rhythm" and step to the *quarter-note* pulse to outline the *"three-feel."* Count 16th notes, clapping the stressed beats: "**1**e&a-**2**e&a-**3**e&a," to feel the four-over-three pulse. In this example, the polyrhythms are simply played *half* as fast (Letter A) and *twice* as fast (Letter C) as the "root rhythm." These polyrhythms are the foundations for all the studies that follow. Interpret them spiritedly, using a variety of stickings and limb combinations, and "make them dance."

Practice Tips

The *Progressive Hemiola Combination in 4/4* (pg. 63), is the *polyrhythmic* alternative to the traditional method of opening and closing a long roll, while *Overlapping Roundtable Form* (pg. 64), compresses and expands the STT simultaneously between the hands and feet. *Hemiola Ostinatos I: Subdividing Meter* (pg. 65), employs 4-way coordination by executing a polyrhythm with the feet and applying timetable combinations to the "root" pulse with the hands, while *Hemiola Ostinatos II: Subdividing Polymeter* (pg. 68), then applies them, as indicated, to the pulse of the polymeter.

Basic Polyrhythms Defined by Meter

1. 3:2 in 4/4

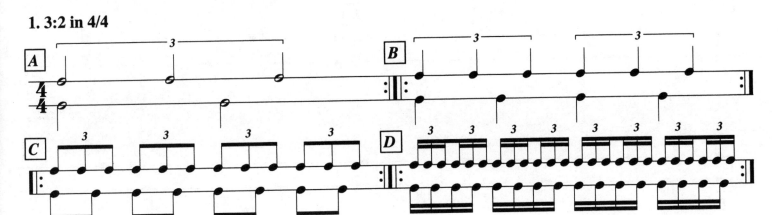

2. 2:3 in 3/4

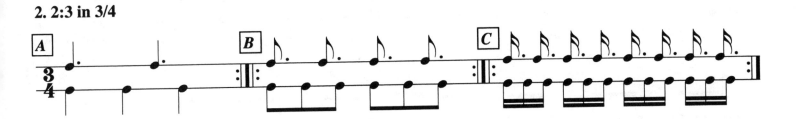

3. 3:4 in 4/4

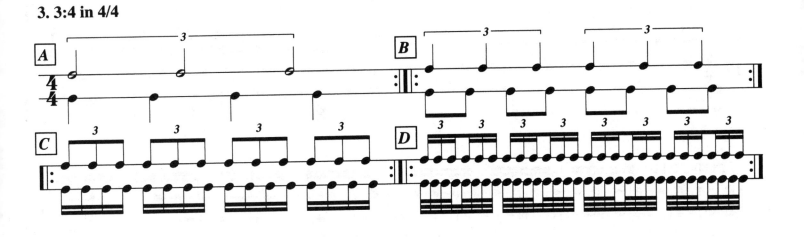

4. 4:3 in 3/4

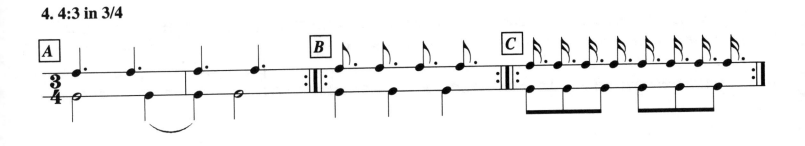

Progressive Hemiola Combination in 4/4

Overlapping Roundtable Form

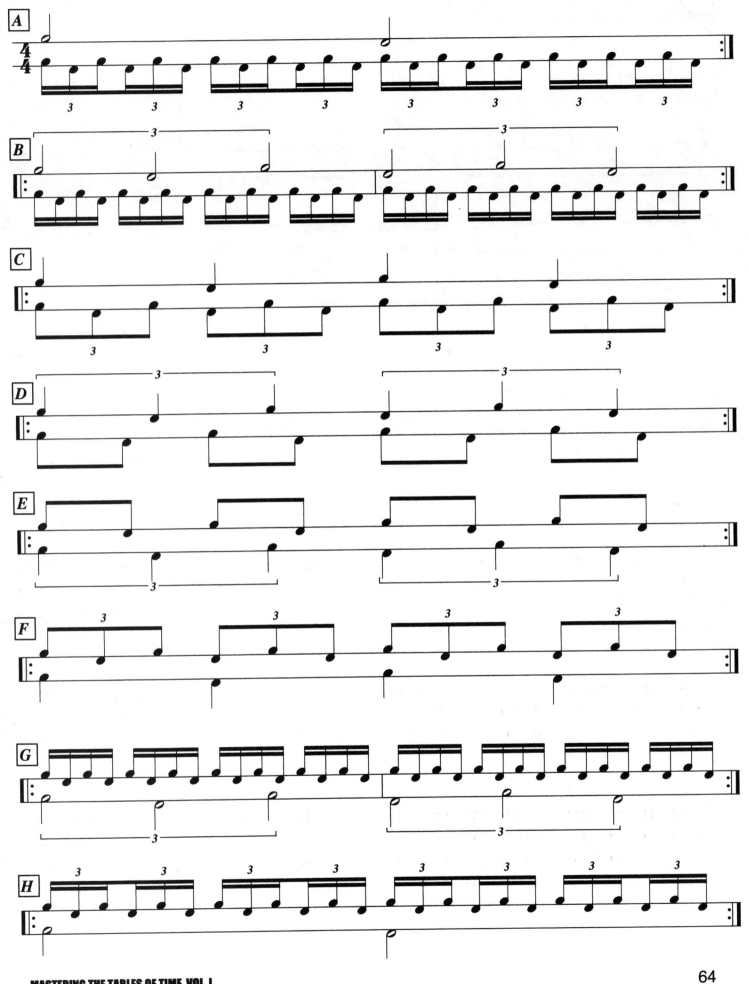

Hemiola Ostinatos I: Subdividing Meter

1. 3:2 A

2. 3:2 B

3. 2:3 A

65

4. 2:3 B

5. 3:4 A

6. 3:4 B

7. 4:3 A

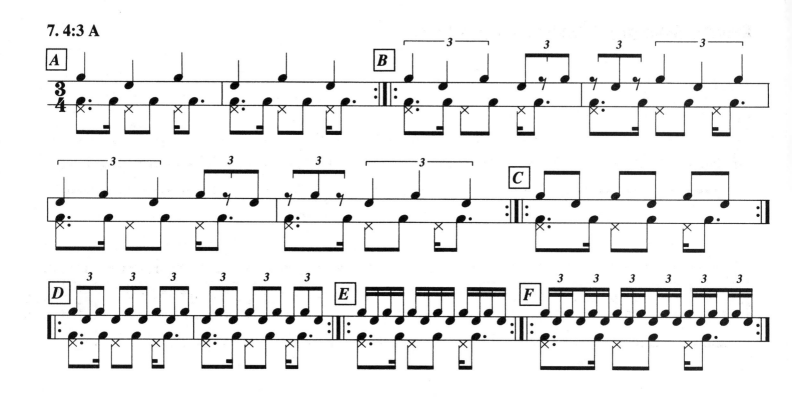

8. 4:3 B

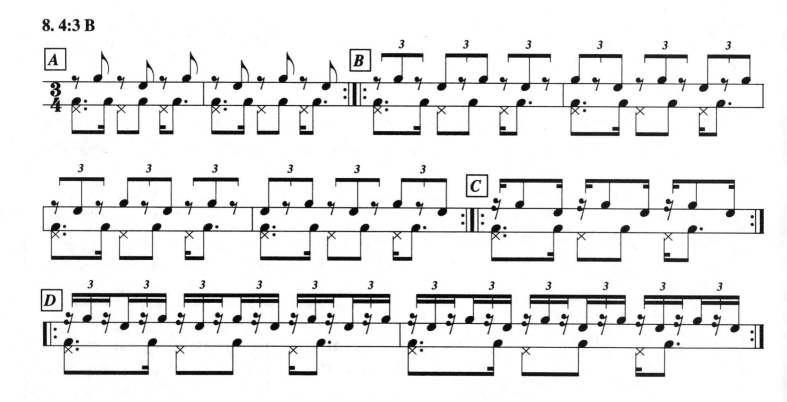

Hemiola Ostinatos II: Subdividing Polymeter

1. 3:2 A

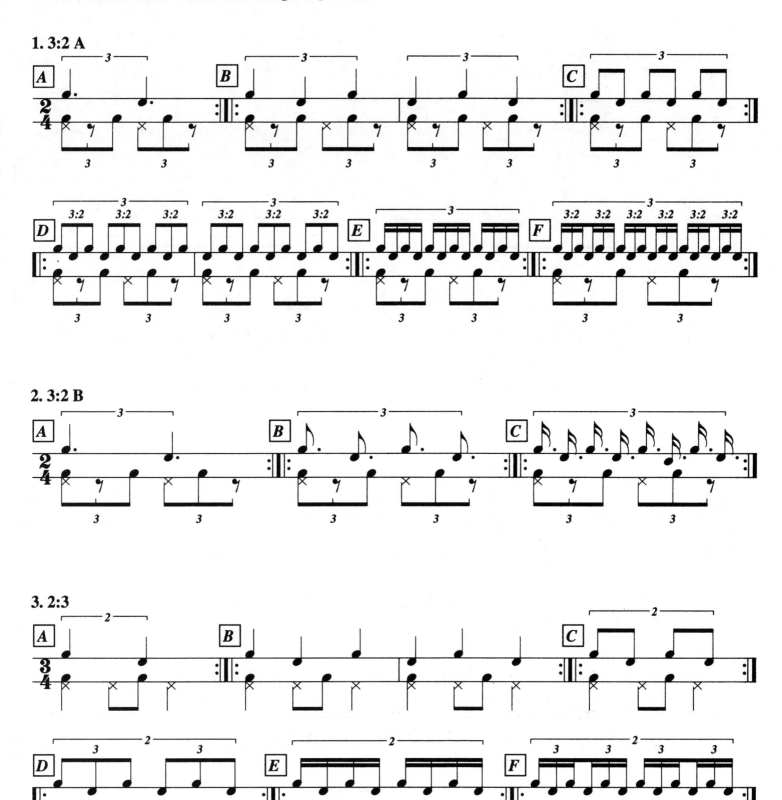

2. 3:2 B

3. 2:3

4. 3:4

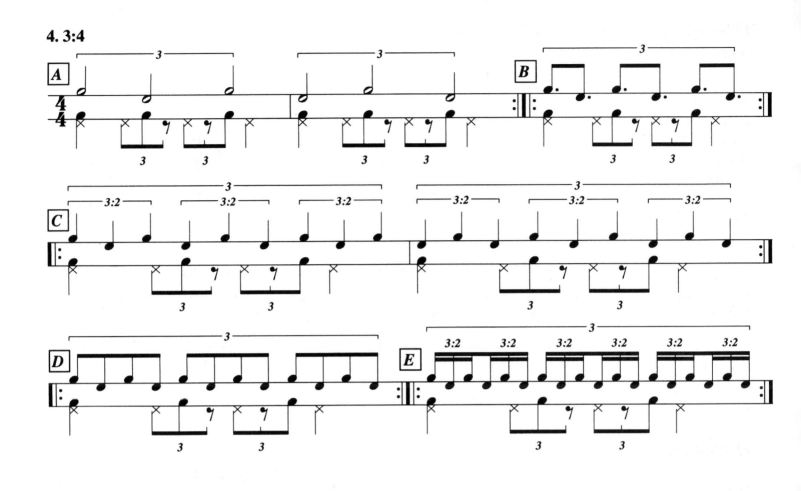

5. 4:3

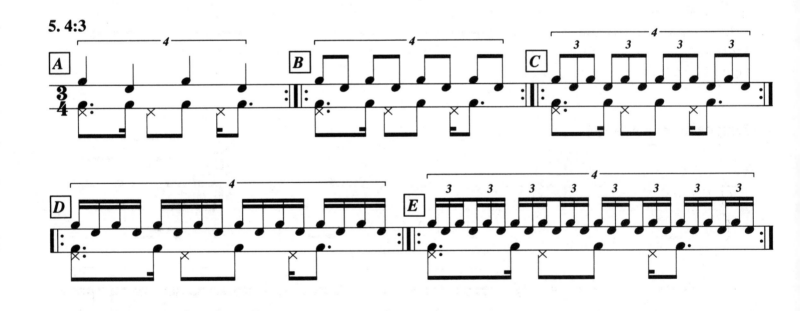

Part Three: Determining Tempo through Metric Modulation

Have you ever witnessed a conductor intently studying his or her wristwatch prior to rehearsing a new piece of music, or a session musician doing the same thing while listening to a playback after finishing a take? While it's possible they were just checking for the next union break, it is also likely they were using their timepiece to determine the tempo for the music they're about to play or monitoring the consistency of tempo in one they just recorded.

Application

A *modulation*, in musical terms, is a change of key signature. An example would be the bridge of a pop tune that might commonly be based around the IV chord of the original key, rather than the I chord. A *metric* modulation then refers to a change of meter, or time signature, in which a new subdivision or polyrhythm is introduced to take on the role of the "new quarter-note pulse." This change of meter can be either actual, where the time signature in a composition changes, or *implied*, creating the feel of a new meter over the original pulse, which is retained throughout. The timetable below illustrates subdivisions for determining "new quarter-note pulses," at a variety of tempos, by using any timepiece with a second hand, or digital display thereof, based on the foundation of quarter-note = 60 beats per minute (one beat per second).

Practice Tips

Memorize three consecutive tempo-to-subdivision grouping ratios: the original quarter-note pulse = 60 bpm (Letter D), the dotted-eighth pulse (roughly 1.333 times faster) = 80 bpm (Letter E), and the quarter-note triplet pulse (1.5 times faster) = 90 bpm (Letter F). Then you can easily calculate tempos half, twice, or three times as fast for each, using simple division or multiplication. Apply two, three, or four-note sticking combinations to any subdivision defining a new tempo to feel the pulse of the time signature you desire.

Tempos Determined by Subdivision   (based on ♩ = 60 bpm)

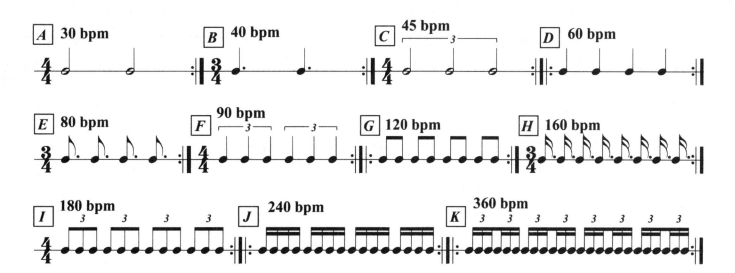

As purveyors of the almighty groove, it could be said that syncopation is our occupation. The backbeat, which can be clinically defined as the stressing of beats 2 and 4, typically on the snare drum, is synonymous with the definition of syncopation. Syncopation shifts the emphasis from accenting a typically strong downbeat pulse (beats 1 and 3, in 4/4) to the normally weaker upbeat pulse. The pendulum-like balance of the downbeat/backbeat continuum is less regimented in feel with an emphasis on the backbeat, instilling the urge to dance rather than march, which is why the backbeat generally sits atop the mix of sounds in contemporary groove music.

Application

Our focus is on applying subdivisions to groove ostinatos with a consistent backbeat, on beats 2 and 4, in common time. The bass drum is often called the *"mother drum"* due to its importance in defining the foundation and balance every groove needs, and so the *Progressions for Single/Double Bass Drum* are applied to the most common of ostinatos: the 8/8 and 12/8 pulses. While written for single bass drum they can easily be interpreted for double bass as well. Note that in the 12/8 pulses, the "middle-note" of each 8th note triplet played on the cymbal is shown in parenthesis. It can be played or *omitted*–to create the option of a *shuffle-feel*–for those examples. Also note that all subdivision variations for the *12/8 pulse* contain "swung" interpretations of the 8th and 16th note rhythms (as well as "straight" ones) as they are commonly applied in this manner to triplet phrasing.

The *Progressions for Hi Hat/Ride Cymbal in 4/4 Time* (pg. 77), and *Accent Progressions for Hi Hat/Ride Cymbal in Standard Subdivisions* (pg. 78), move the subdivision phrasing to the RH over a basic downbeat/backbeat continuum. Subdividing with the LF is the focus of the *Hi-Hat/Foot Counterpoint* studies on pg. 80. In these examples, the ostinatos incorporate first a downbeat pulse in the RH, and are then repeated with an upbeat pulse. These variations highlight great syncopation and tone color options when played by the RH on the hi-hat as well as the ride cymbal. The RH and LF then work together to execute the funky syncopation of the two, three and four-note sequences of the *Open/Close Phrasing Progressions for Hi Hat w/Hand & Foot* (pg. 82). The chapter concludes with *Advanced Ostinato Combinations I* and *II*. *Combination I* focuses on a basic 8/8 groove in which the RH executes both the HH and SD parts, freeing the LH to play counterpoint subdivisions. *Combination II* reverses the roles of the hands with an upbeat 8th and backbeat HH/SD combination in the LH and counterpoint in the RH.

Practice Tips

It is not uncommon to also play backbeats on beat 3 of the bar to create a half time feel, the upbeat 8th notes ("&'s"), to create a double-time feel, or even four-to-the-bar on the downbeats–a staple of the classic "Motown Sound" in pop music. Applying these backbeat variations, as well as different bass drum and/or cymbal rhythms from the *Counterpoint Ostinato Options* (pg. 25), to the timetables, where appropriate, enhances your options and overall versatility for finding the "right" groove for any occasion.

Progressions for Single/Double Bass Drum ~ 8/8 Pulse

1. Standard Subdivisions

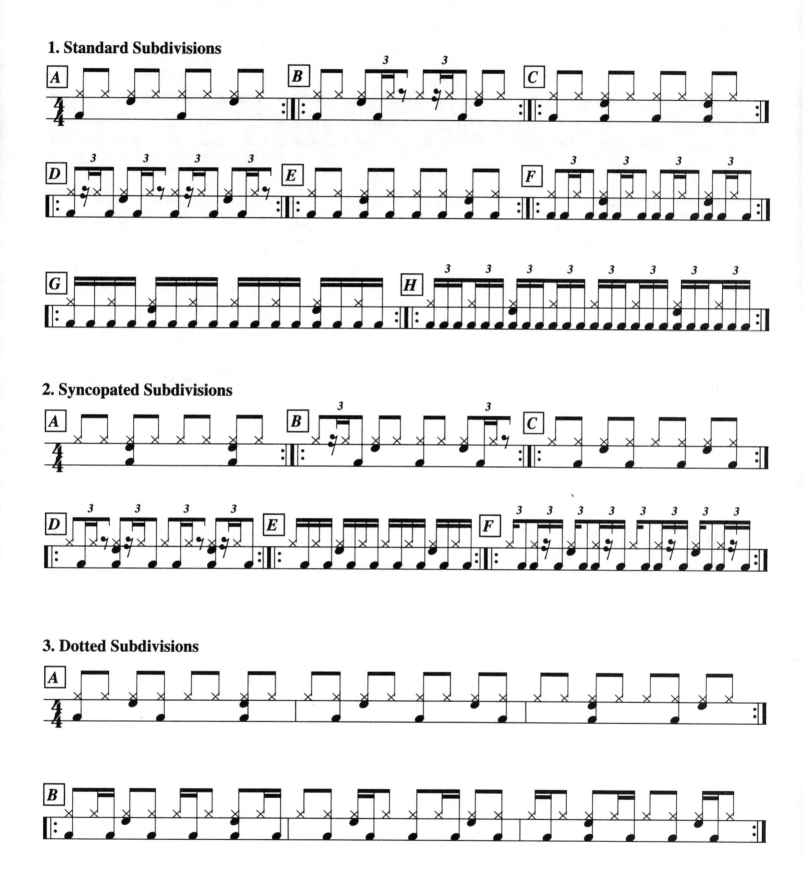

2. Syncopated Subdivisions

3. Dotted Subdivisions

4. Dotted Motive I

5. Dotted Motive II

6. Dotted Motive III

Progressions for Single/Double Bass Drum ~ 12/8 Pulse

1. Standard Subdivisions

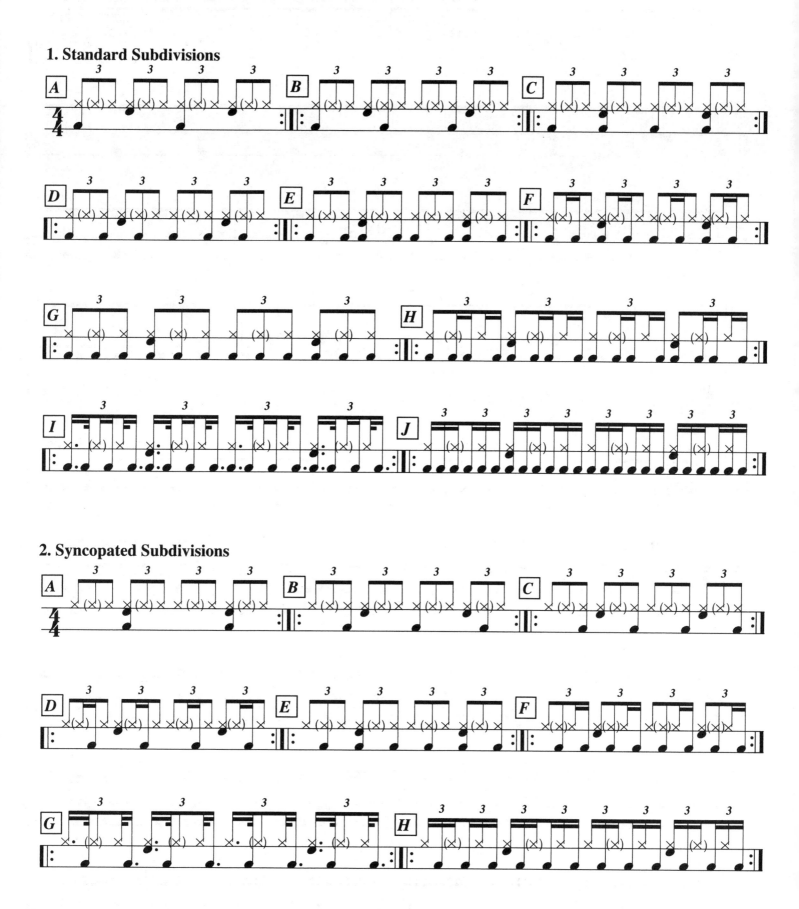

2. Syncopated Subdivisions

3. Dotted Subdivisions

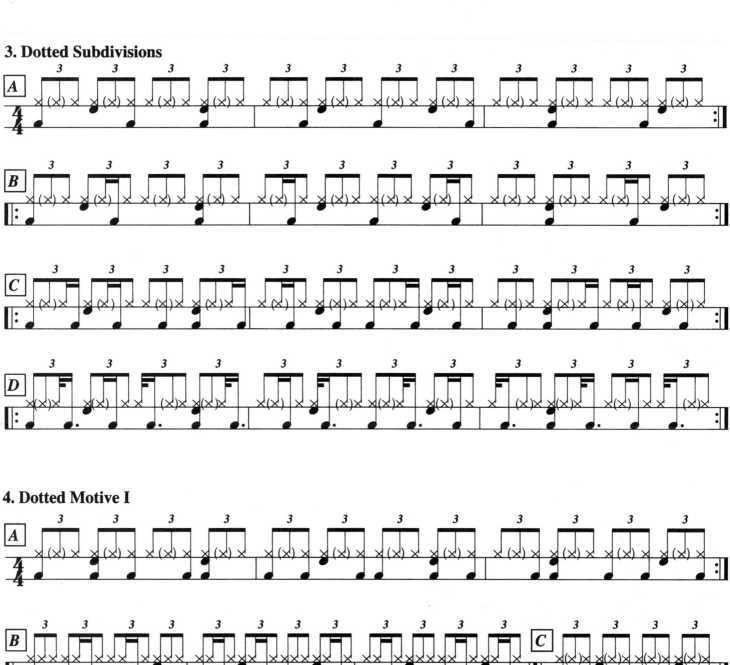

4. Dotted Motive I

5. Dotted Motive II

6. Dotted Motive III

Progressions for Hi-Hat/Ride Cymbal in 4/4 Time

1. Standard Subdivisions

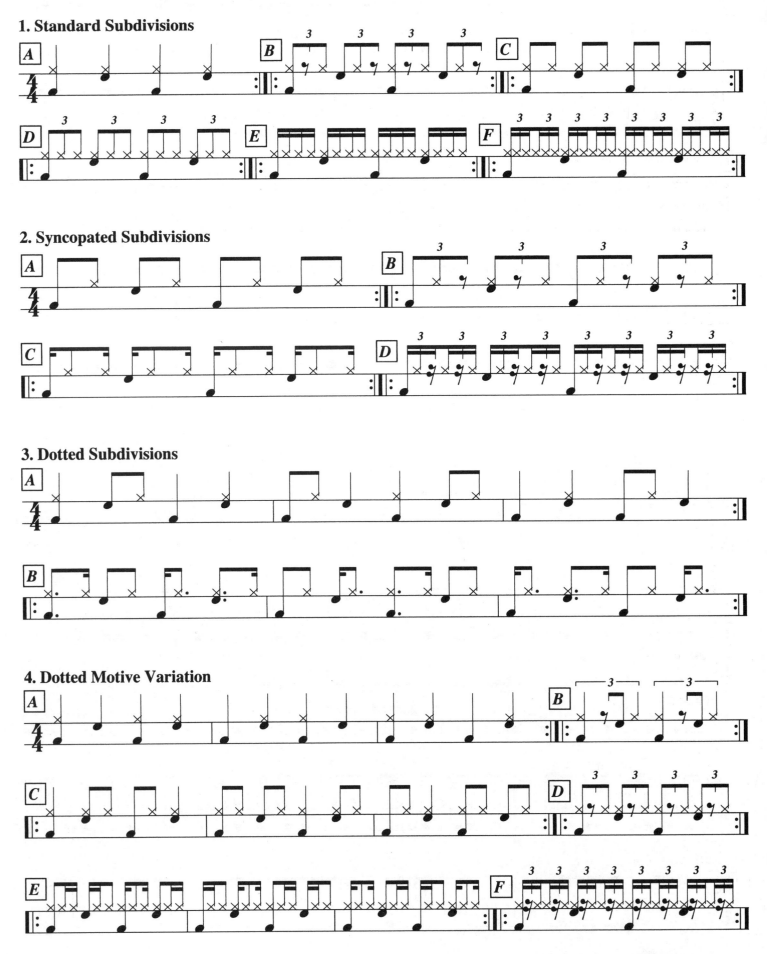

2. Syncopated Subdivisions

3. Dotted Subdivisions

4. Dotted Motive Variation

Accent Progressions for Hi-Hat/Ride Cymbal in Standard Subdivisions

1. Two-Note Accent Grouping I

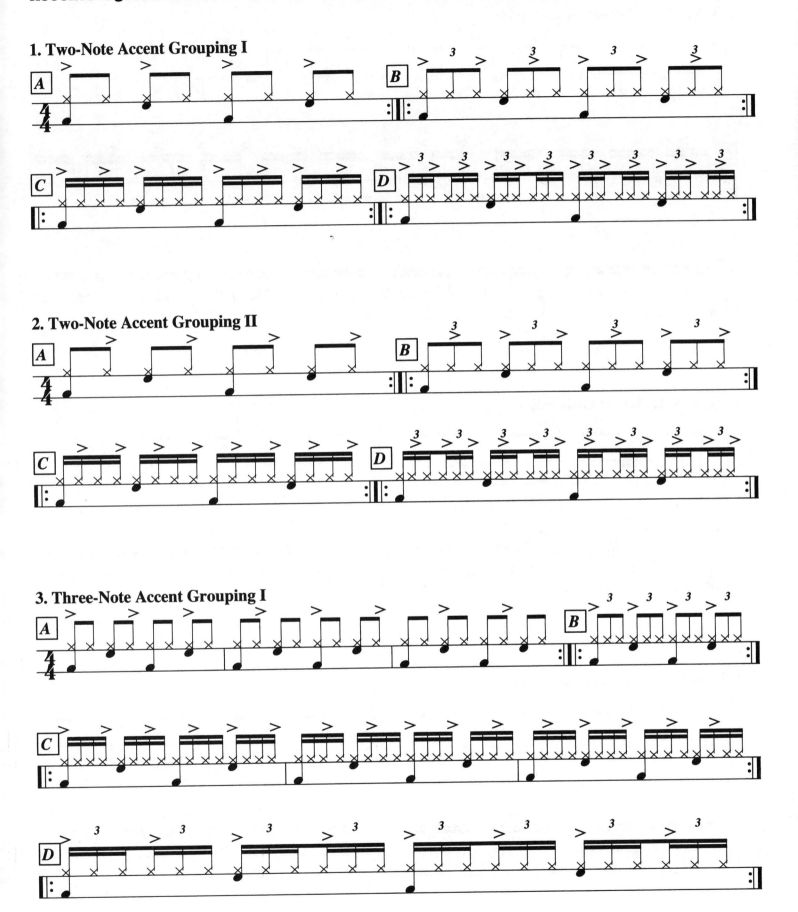

2. Two-Note Accent Grouping II

3. Three-Note Accent Grouping I

4. Three-Note Accent Grouping II

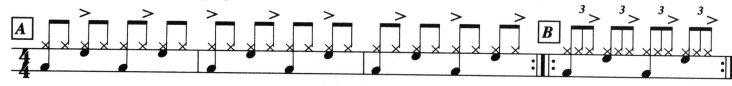

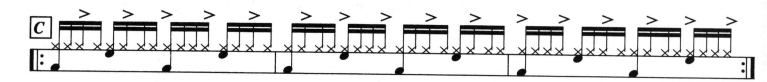

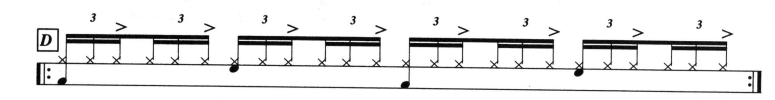

5. Four-Note Accent Grouping I

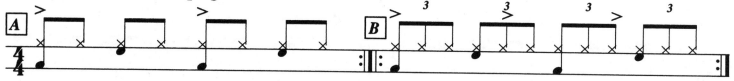

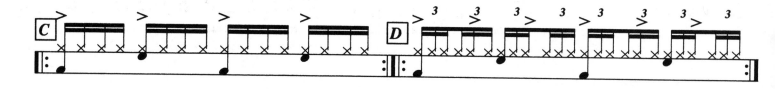

6. Four-Note Accent Grouping II

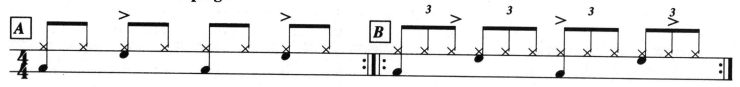

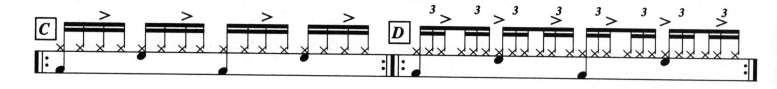

Hi-Hat/Foot Counterpoint

1. Standard Subdivisions I

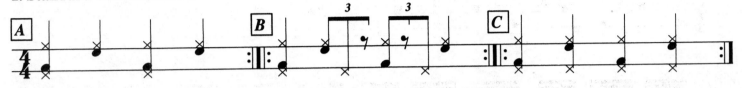

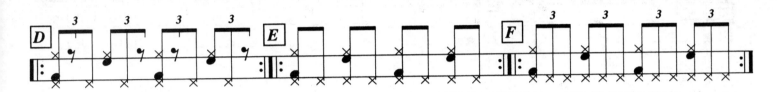

2. Syncopated Subdivisions I

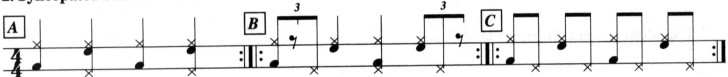

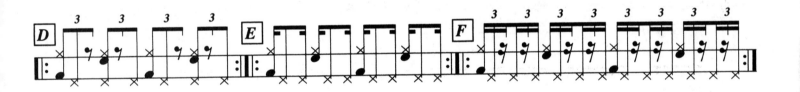

3. Dotted Subdivisions I

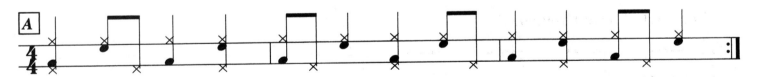

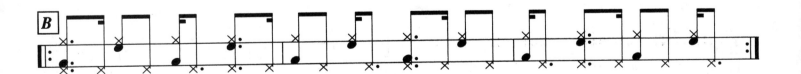

4. Standard Subdivisions II

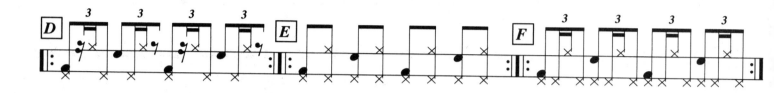

5. Syncopated Subdivisions II

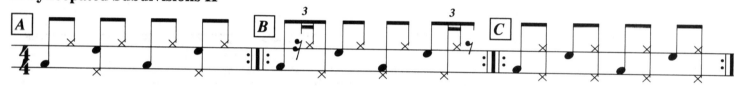

6. Dotted Subdivisions II

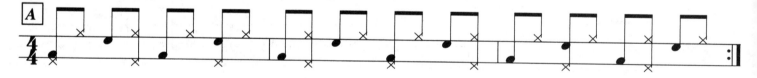

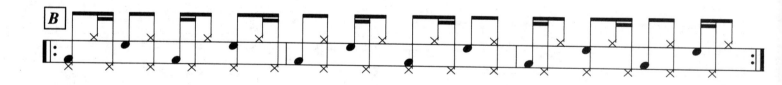

81

Open/Close Phrasing Progressions for Hi-Hat w/Hand & Foot

1. Two-Note Sequence (Root Position)

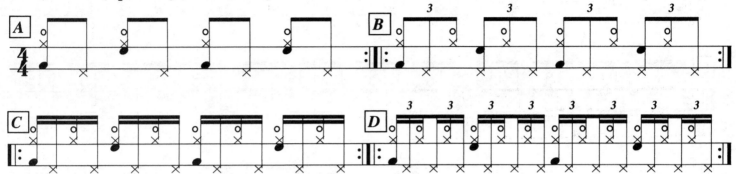

2. Two-Note Sequence (Inverted)

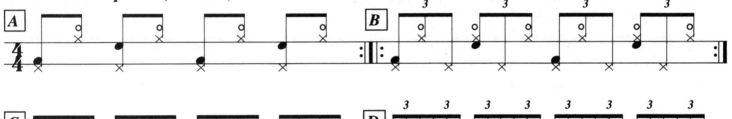
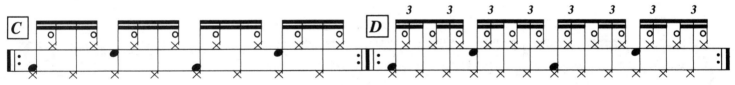

3. Three-Note Sequence (Root Position)

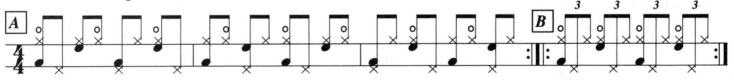
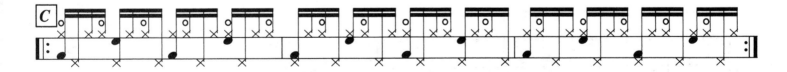
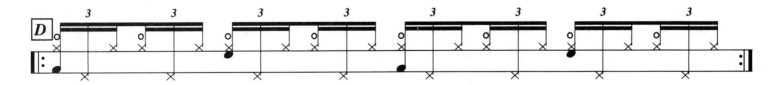

4. Three-Note Sequence (1st Inversion)

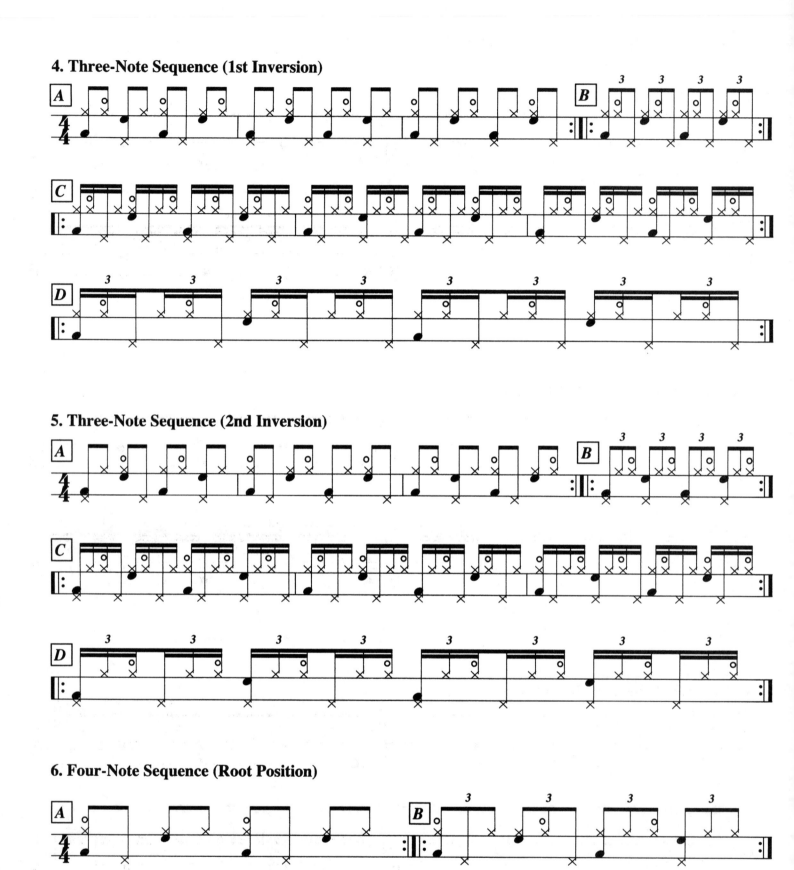

5. Three-Note Sequence (2nd Inversion)

6. Four-Note Sequence (Root Position)

7. Four-Note Sequence (1st Inversion)

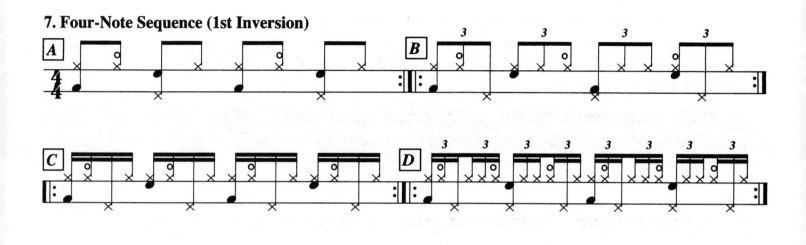

8. Four-Note Sequence (2nd Inversion)

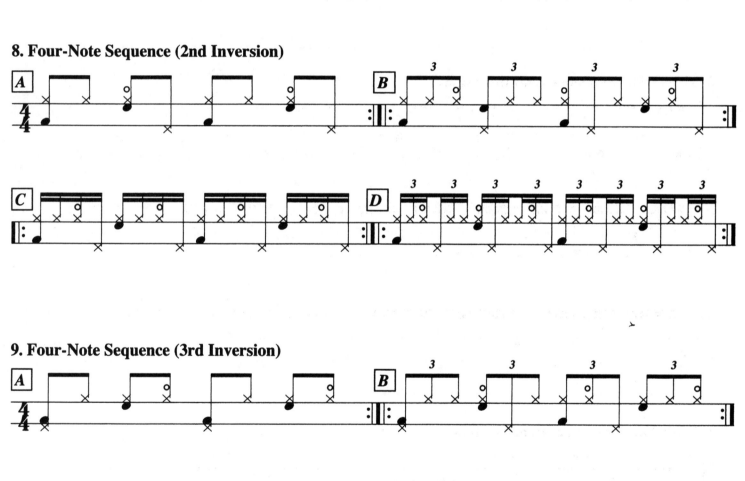

9. Four-Note Sequence (3rd Inversion)

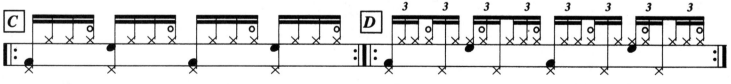

Advanced Ostinato Combination I: RH/RF w/LH Counterpoint

1. Standard Subdivisions

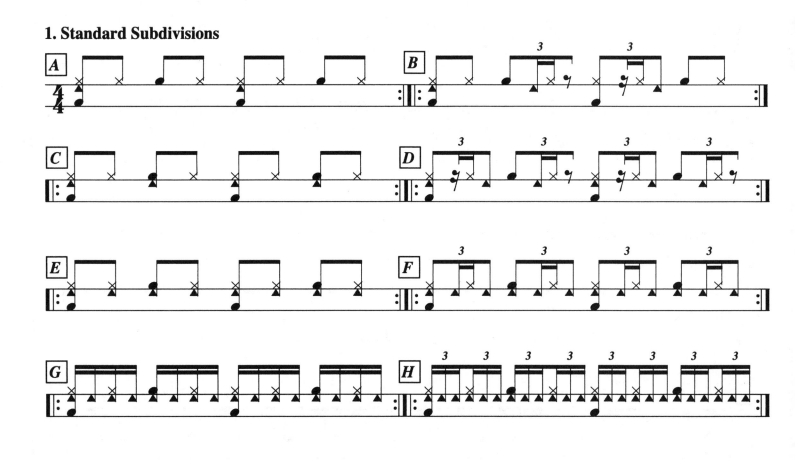

2. Syncopated Subdivisions

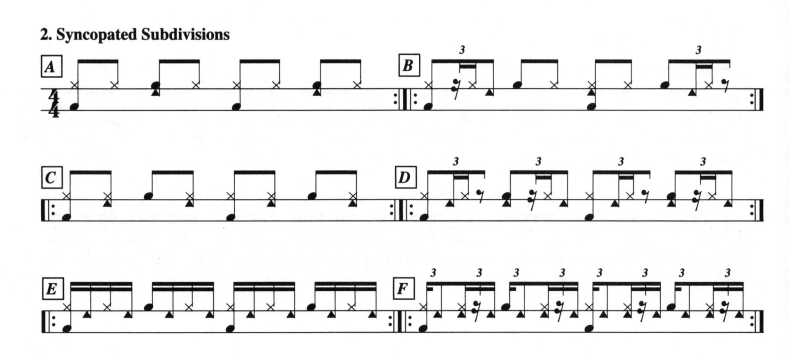

3. Dotted Subdivisions

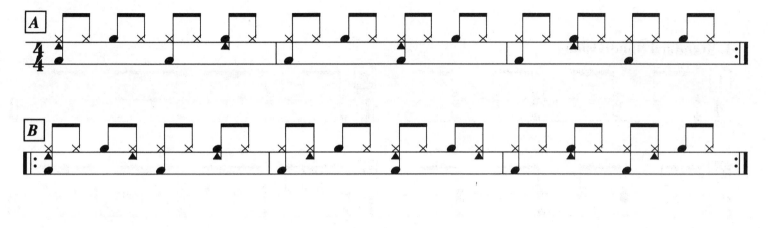

4. Dotted Motive Variation

Advanced Ostinato Combination II: LH/RF w/RH Counterpoint

1. Standard Subdivisions

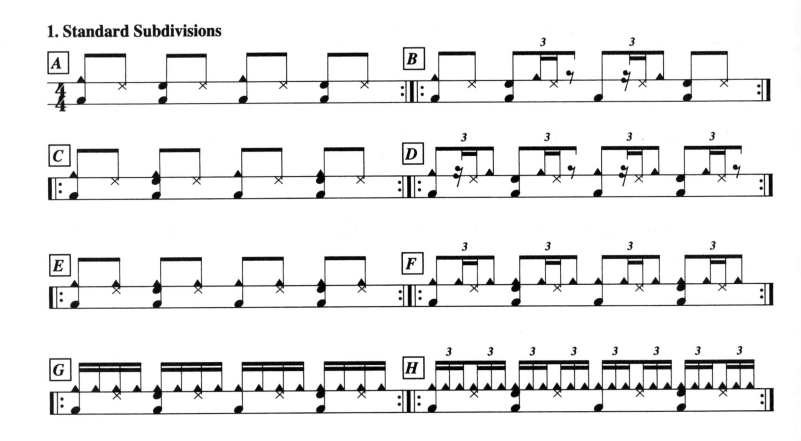

2. Syncopated Subdivisions

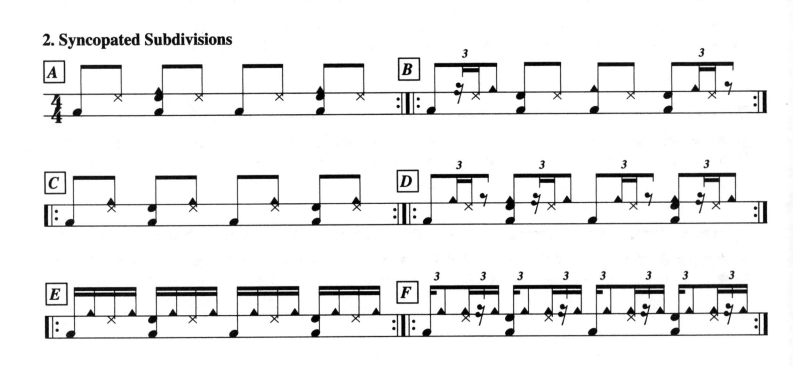

3. Dotted Subdivisions

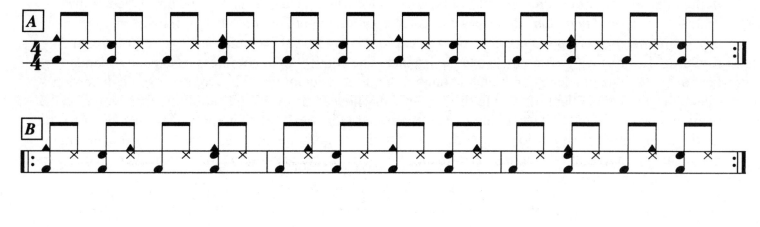

4. Dotted Motive Variation

In the rich folklore of the crescent city of New Orleans, which is also arguably the birthplace of the drumset, the word *"mujician"* describes a musician possessing the talent to perform magically, as if beyond human skill. The *Modulations Studies* explored here reveal "secrets," as it were, for creating rhythmic illusions with which to dazzle the listener. The concept is to compress or expand a standard beat over subdivisions both common and uncommon to its general use. This creates a sonic distortion that is the aural equivalent of "seeing the beat in a fun-house mirror." When applying this "voodoo," be warned: once mastered this technique must be conjured judiciously, with great discretion and taste. The modulations introduce a tension to the music that typically goes against-the-grain of the groove, which can create not only *excitement* in a performance but potentially *confusion* as well, to dancers, listeners and your fellow musicians.

Application

The *Implied Metric Modulation Progressions* on the following page provide a primer in ear training and timekeeping to develop the solid foundation necessary for properly executing the modulations. They also, in examples 1-6, illustrate common musical applications of creating half-time, double-time, and related feels, over a variety of cymbal ostinato rhythms, depending on where the backbeat is placed. Note that the *Quarter-Note* and 8th *Note Progressions* each feature two common sticking options: *"hand and hand"* (RH on cymbal or HH, LH on SD), followed by *"hand to hand"* (alternate sticking for HH/SD). Example 6 begins the series of applying beats to the *Standard Timetable*. Letter C is its "root rhythm" (see *Glossary of Terms*, pg. 135). In example 7, note that the *8/16 Pulse* is based on a "root rhythm" played twice inside Letter E. The *8/16 Pulse* has a timeline lasting the length of beats 1 through 2, and simply recycles on beats 3 and 4. 8/16 then refers to one revolution of the cycle (as in 2/4) and Letter E is the foundation for playing Letters A-D, and F, with the proper interpretation. Examples 8 and 9 illustrate the 12/8 pulse, and its shuffle variation, as applied to the *Standard Timetable*.

Advanced applications, presented as a series of *Theme & Variation* studies, close out the chapter. The *Paradiddle Funk Groove Progressions* (pg. 93), expand on the syncopated and natural backbeats inherent to these rudiments. *Modulating Traditional Grooves* (pg. 95), explores modulating three classic beats (and one riff, in example 3), common to the vocabulary of the drumset. So too are the *Linear "Bo Diddley Beat" Adaptations* (pg. 97), which utilize an *abstraction*, in that they feature duple variations at Letter A, and "fattened-up" triple variations at Letter B throughout. These each then compress into a double-time feel at Letters C and D. The *Flam Rudiments with Afro/Latin Beat Influence* (pg. 98), are *not* backbeat rhythms per se, but they *are* funky, *and* offer both an example of interpreting flam studies around the drumset, and a preview of the type of *World Beat Groove Studies* that will be explored in *Volume II* of *Mastering the Tables of Time*.

Practice Tips

Use the examples presented in this section as a template for applying your imagination to develop your own interpretations. Lock in and play with feeling and conviction!

Implied Metric Modulation Progressions

1. Quarter Note Progression ~ Hand & Hand

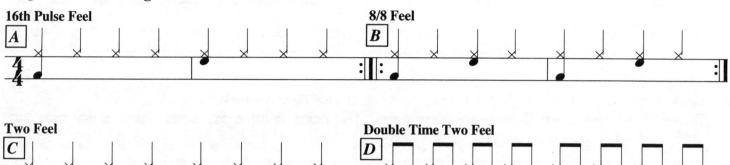

2. Quarter Note Progression ~ Hand to Hand

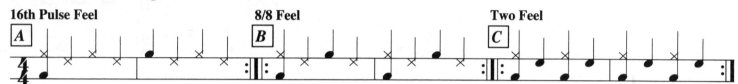

3. 8th Note Progression ~ Hand & Hand

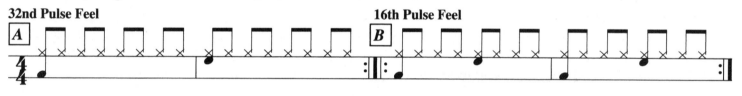

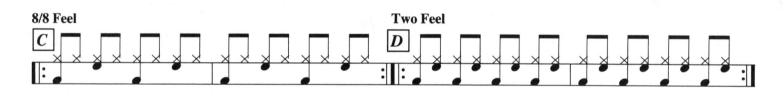

4. 8th Note Progression ~ Hand to Hand

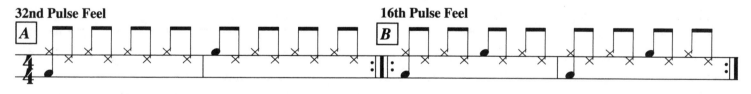

5. Offbeat 8th Note Progression

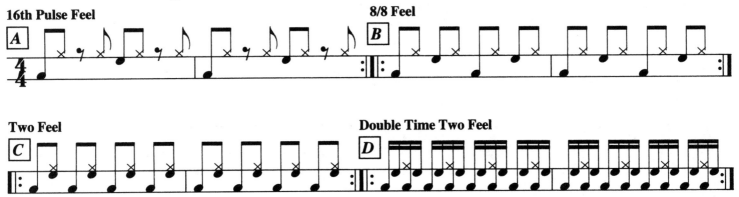

6. 8/8 Pulse Progression in Standard Subdivisions

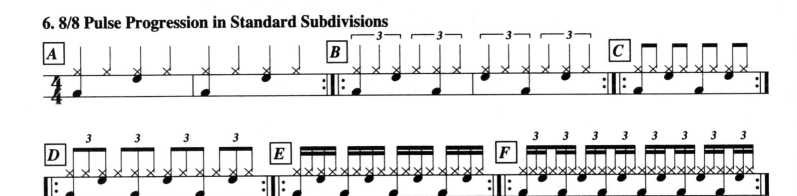

7. 8/16 Pulse Progression in Standard Subdivisions

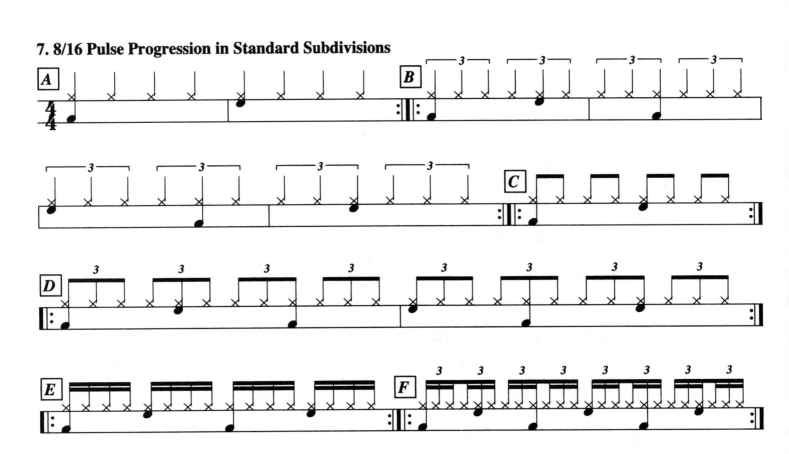

8. 12/8 Pulse Progression in Standard Subdivisions I

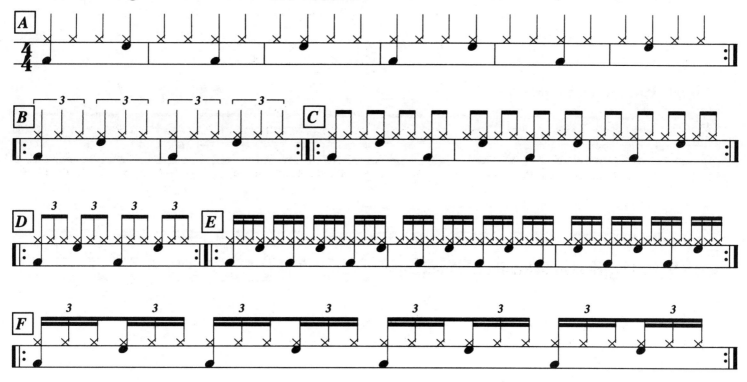

9. 12/8 Pulse Progression in Standard Subdivisions II (Shuffle Variation)

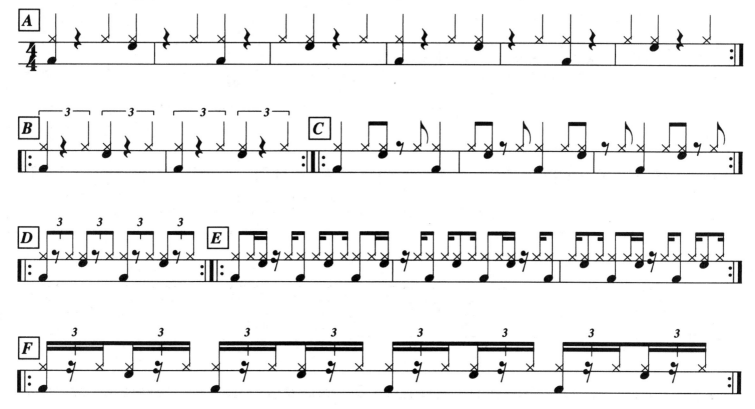

Theme & Variation I: Paradiddle Funk Groove Progressions

1. Single Paradiddle Variation

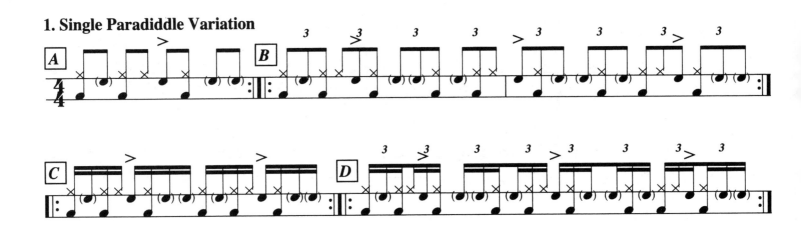

2. Double Paradiddle Variation

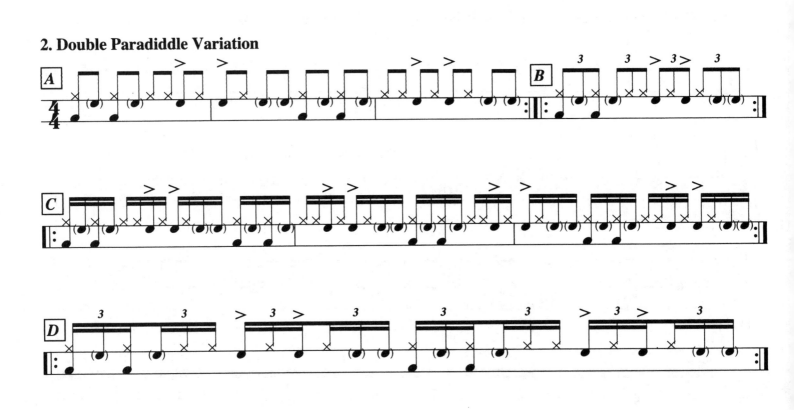

3. Paradiddle-diddle Variation

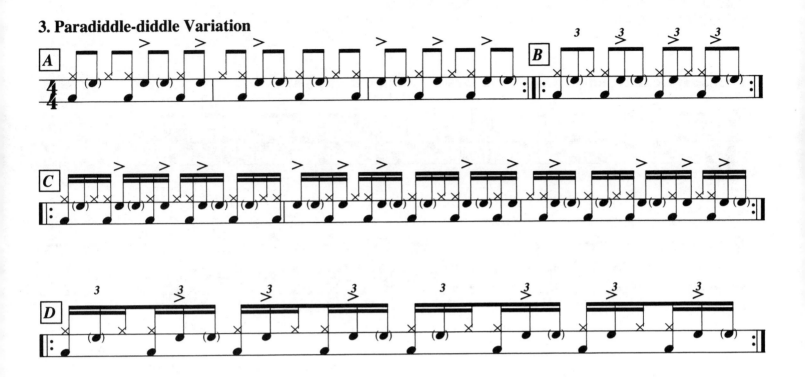

4. Triple Paradiddle Variation

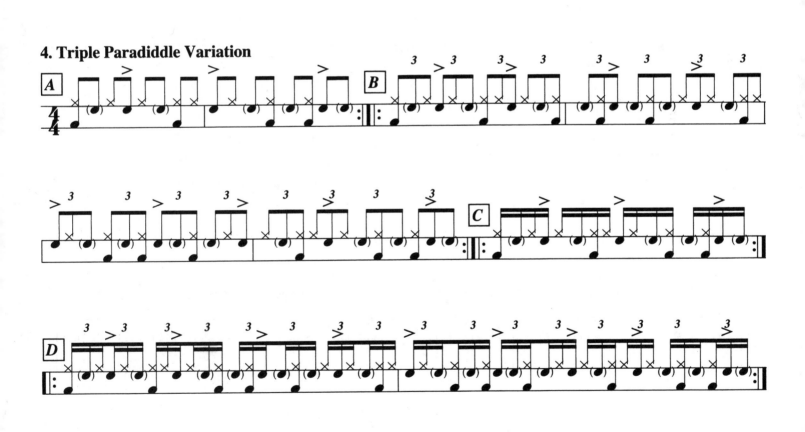

Theme & Variation II: Modulating Traditional Grooves

1. Cajun "Double Clutch"/Country & Western "Train Beat" Variation

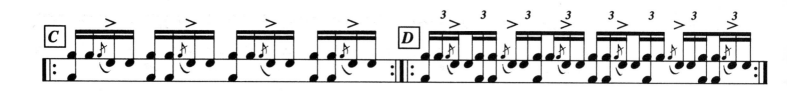

2. The Funky "King Kong" Beat Variation

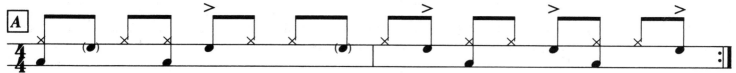

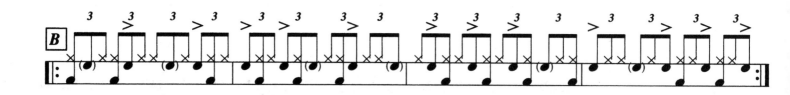

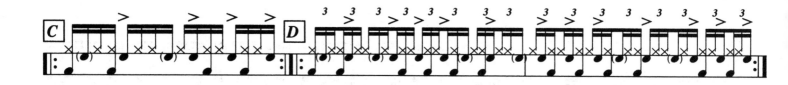

3. Four-Stroke Ruff Variation as Applied to Drum & Bass/Rhythm & Blues

4. The "Boogaloo" Variation

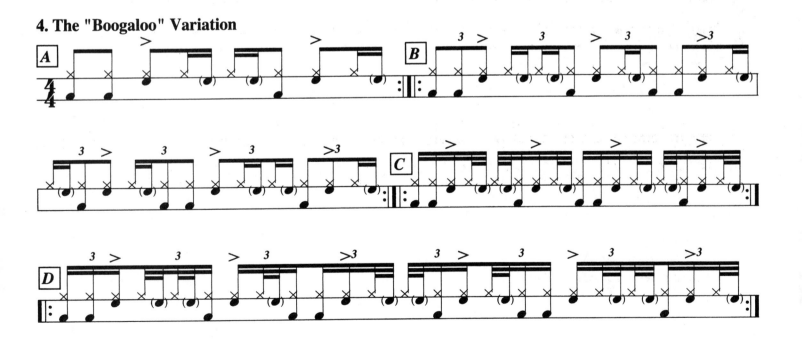

Theme & Variation III: Linear "Bo Diddley Beat" Adaptations

1. Basic Variations

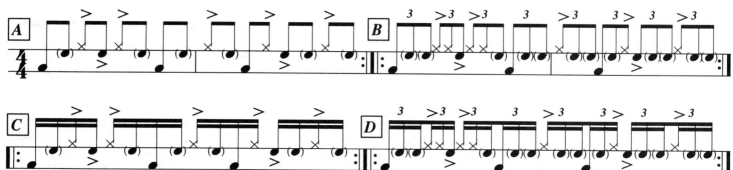

2. Advanced Variations

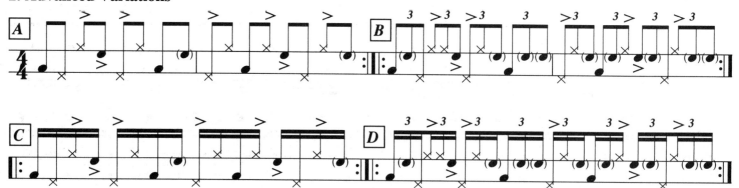

3. "Street Beat" Variations*

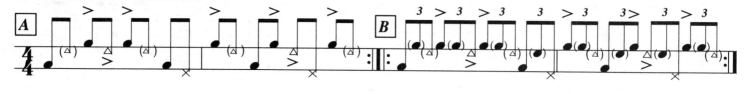

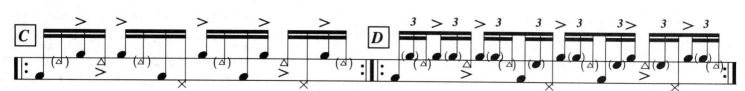

* **Letters B & D:**
  SD ghost notes in RH = stick
  SD ghost notes in LH = finger taps

Theme & Variation IV: Flam Rudiments with Afro/Latin Beat Influence

1. Pataflafla/Brazilian "Jazz Samba" Variation

2. Swiss Windmill/New Orleans "Street Beat" Variation

3. Flam Accent (Root Position)/African Bell Rhythm Variation

The musical art of Jazz, born in the USA, in the early 20th Century, also gave birth to the drumset. The bass drum pedal allowed one person to play both the downbeat and the backbeat in a 2/4 *ragtime* style that combined European concert drums and rudimental tradition with polyrhythms indigenous to the descendants of African culture who then defined this new style and instrument. In the *Swing Era*, the pulse evolved into a strong "four-on-the-floor" foundation with a more swung 8th subdivision. As mid-century approached the *be-bop* drummers redefined the rhythmic expression, shifting the timekeeping foundation from the bass drum and snare drum to the ride cymbal and hi-hat. This lighter emphasis of the downbeat/backbeat pulse well suited the phrasing and faster tempos of the style. It also opened the door for more syncopation to be utilized within the groove–a unique approach that has remained standard in jazz drumming and is the foundation for the following studies.

Application

This section focuses on the art of "comping" within the groove, a form of conversational accompaniment used while backing an improvising soloist. It is also useful for "catching" rhythmic figures in melodies or arrangements, and even soloing "inside the groove." "Swung" *abstractions* of all 8th note subdivisions are included (along with "straight"), as this pulse is the foundation of jazz phrasing. The cymbal rhythm's *offbeat* varies in both *notation*, as swung 8/8 or dotted $8^{th}/16^{th}$ (depending on the subdivision in use), and *feel* (as with *two* vs. *four* feels, for example). Keep the cymbal beat relaxed, yet driving. The *swing* of the cymbal beat is the focal point the comping must balance around.

Play all *One Voice Comping* studies with SD then BD, to lay the foundation for conversing *between* the two drums. This concept is applied in all *Two-Voice Comping* studies as follows: *The Standard and Syncopated Progressions* (pg. 100) show common rudimental phrasing between the drums (try also reversing the voicings). The *Dotted Pulse/Motive Progressions* (pg. 103) use rhythmic vocabulary, common to jazz phrasing, based on riffs from music by Duke Ellington, Dizzy Gillespie, and Lester Young. The *Hi-Hat/Foot Counterpoint* studies (pg. 106) use standard, syncopated, and dotted subdivisions to offer comping alternatives to the backbeat function of the hi-hat, and "break-up" the groove. Try also playing the LF/HH in unison with, or in place of, the BD in all *Two-Voice Comping* studies, *and* simply leaving the LF/HH *tacet* throughout all studies (!).

Practice Tips

The *Hi-Hat/Foot Counterpoint* (pg. 106), and *Dotted Pulse/Motive Progressions* (pg. 103), can be interpreted with a traditional jazz waltz feel by simply playing just the first bar of each 3/4 subdivision, or as written for the longer 6/4 (or implied 4/4) beat. *Brushes* can be applied instead of *sticks* throughout, using a basic RH tap/LH sweep approach: tap the cymbal beat on the SD with the RH. In the LH, use a wide circle to blend the longer notes together for a legato sound, shorten the circle as the notes get smaller, then move to a back and forth, *windshield wiper*-like lateral stroke, and finally a more vertical, stick-like attack, as the notes get smaller still. Do a lot of *listening* and keep it swinging!

Standard and Syncopated Progressions

1. One Voice Comping for SD/BD I

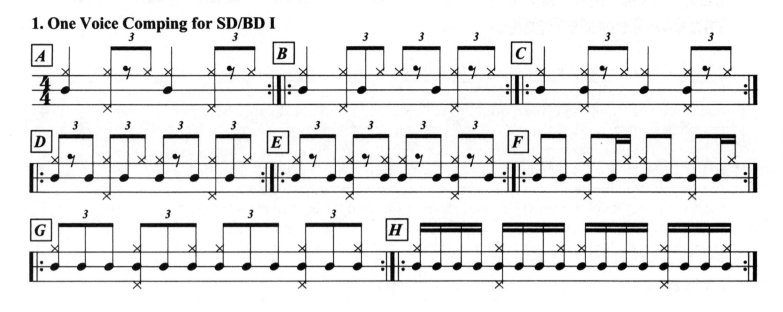

2. One Voice Comping for SD/BD II

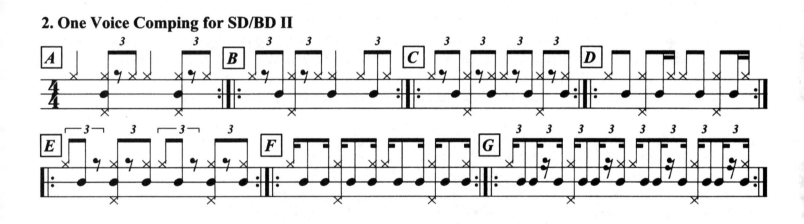

3. Two Voice Comping ~ Single-Stroke Roll I

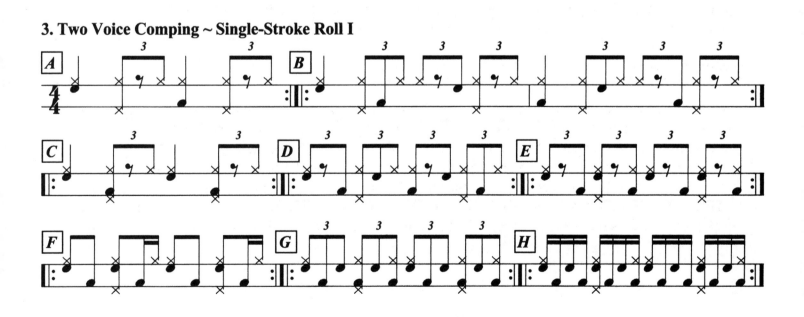

4. Two Voice Comping ~ Single-Stroke Roll II

5. Two Voice Comping ~ Double-Stroke Roll I

6. Two Voice Comping ~ Double-Stroke Roll II

7. Two Voice Comping ~ Inverted Double-Stroke Roll

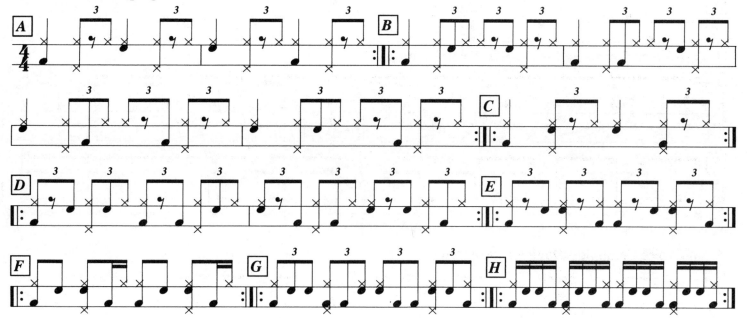

8. Two Voice Comping ~ Single Paradiddle

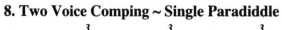

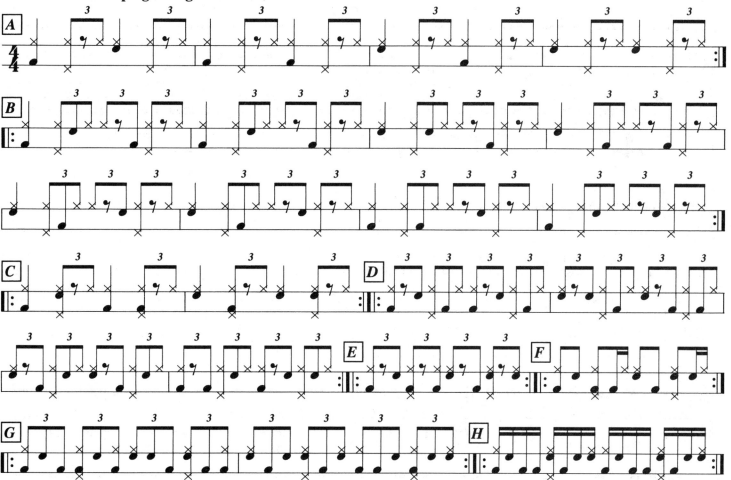

Dotted Pulse / Motive Progressions

1. One Voice Comping for SD/BD (Root Position)

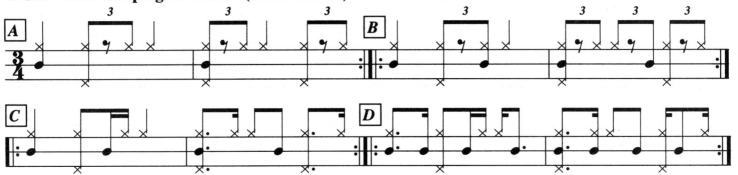

2. One Voice Comping for SD/BD (1st Inversion)

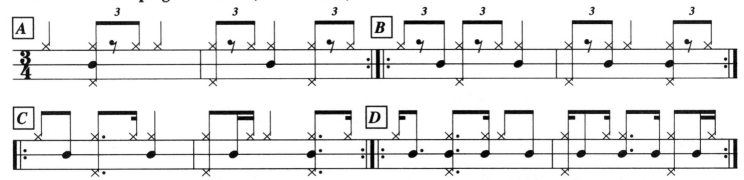

3. One Voice Comping for SD/BD (2nd Inversion)

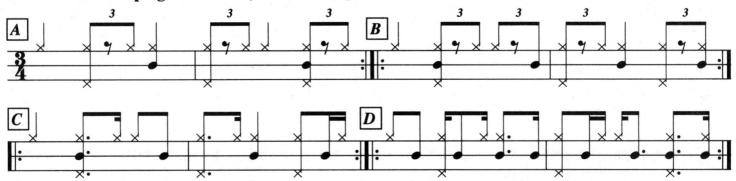

4. One Voice Comping for SD/BD in 4/4

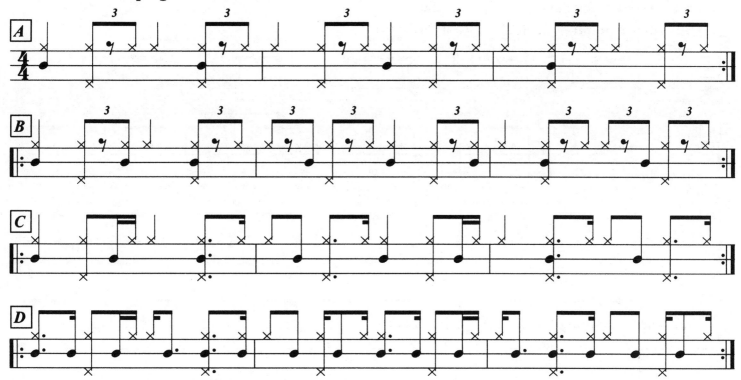

5. Two Voice Riff for SD/BD I ("Doo-Ah, Doo-Ah")

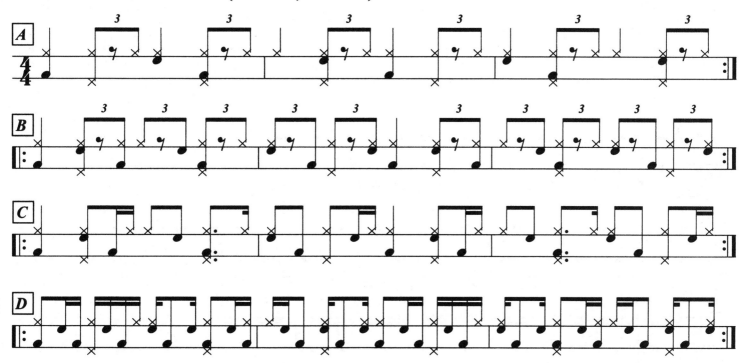

6. Two Voice Riff for SD/BD II ("Salt Peanuts")

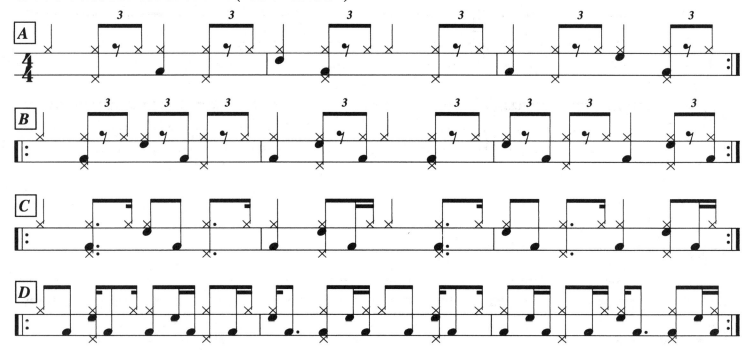

7. Two Voice Riff for SD/BD III ("Ti-Ti-Boom")

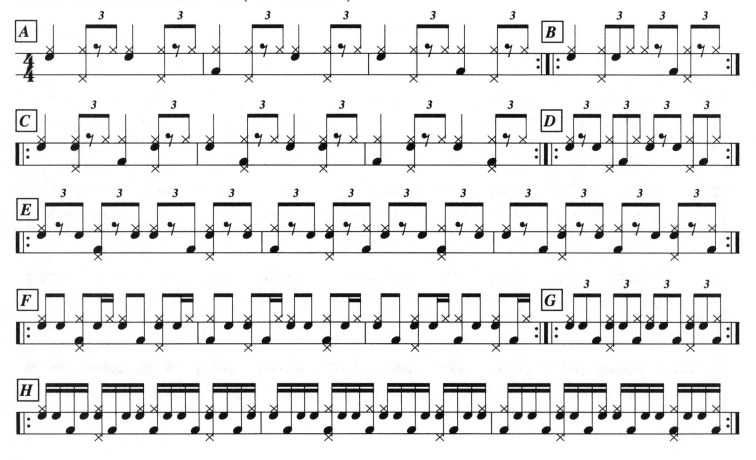

Hi-Hat/Foot Counterpoint

1. 4/4 I

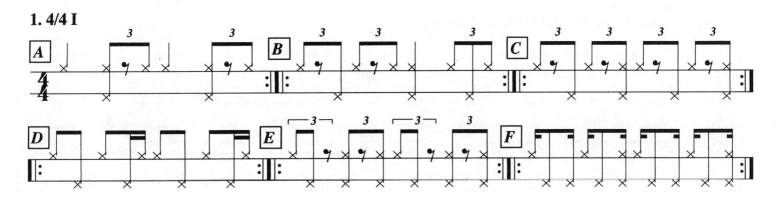

2. 4/4 II

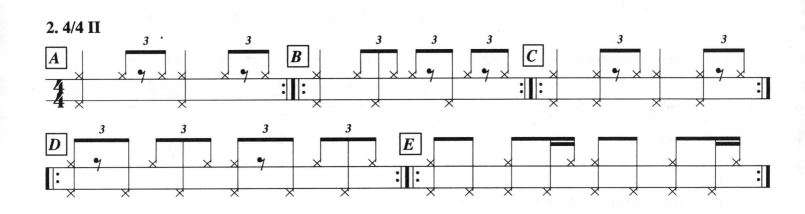

3. 4/4 III

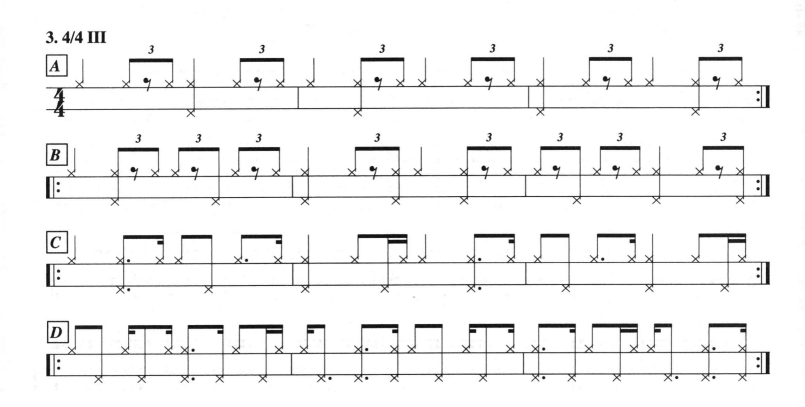

4. 3/4 I (Root Position)

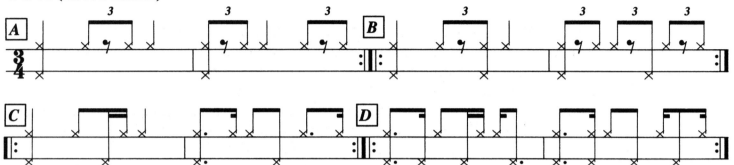

5. 3/4 II (1st Inversion)

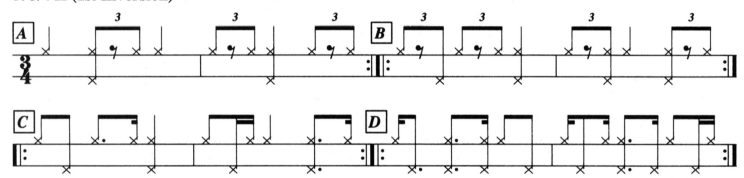

6. 3/4 III (2nd Inversion)

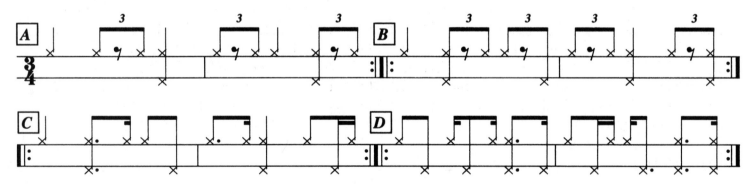

Jazz, as a musical style, is built around the freedom of improvisation and the social concept of democracy in its practice. As the music has evolved, freedom for the drummer has expanded as well. In any musical style, the drummer must provide the proper *feeling* for the music with their *timekeeping*, giving direction through tempo and a sense of *shading* that involves dynamics, velocity, space and the *imagination* to balance these pro-active qualities with a communal interest in *listening* to enhance the "big picture" of the music overall. From the mid-20th Century forward, the influence of world culture introduced new rhythms, odd meters, and advanced polyrhythmic concepts into the language of jazz. The focus on musical freedom of its avant-garde practitioners gave drummers the impetus to expand further on their accompanist role, moving into the front lines of expression through improvisation. A looser, "multi-directional" approach to timekeeping was established and is the focus of the studies presented here.

Application

The *Examples of "Broken-Time" Ride Cymbal Phrasing* (pg. 109) are linear timekeeping modulations, based more on dependent coordination–incorporating hemiola into its sense of forward motion–than the independent coordination applied to the repetitive gallop of the standard cymbal beat in the previous section. They simply compress or expand rhythmically, depending on the direction of flow. These rhythms may not be thought of as rudiment-based by some who play them, but it is useful to see their connection to *Open Drag* and *Four* and *Five-Stroke Ruff* interpretations to illustrate common ground for foundation, form, and function in our playing. All 8th note examples are "straight" vs. "swung" in notation. This way they can easily be interpreted with a shuffled 8th, dotted 8th/16th–or even straighter 8th feel (stylistic in modern-day medium tempos). The LF/HH on 2 and 4 can also vary as described in the previous section.

The *Progressions Combining Standard & Advanced Timekeeping Variations* (pg. 111), are *Abstract Timetables* outlining a progressive order of 4/4 and 3/4 jazz grooves, applied to half, common, and double-time, and implied metric modulations over dotted quarter, dotted 8th, and quarter-note triplet pulses, as well as hemiolas of 2/4 in 3/4, or 3/4 in 4/4. *The Basic Progression in 4/4* (pg. 111) is a primer combining the four basic 4/4 grooves essential in jazz drumming. The *Implied Metric Modulation Progression in 3/4* (pg. 111) introduces the abstract flow in 3/4 time, combining common and implied rhythms in that meter. The *Implied Metric Modulation Progression in 4/4* (pg. 112) shows the "multi-directional" approach in 4/4 time, grounded with a LF/HH foundation on beats 2 and 4 throughout. The *Advanced Implied Metric Modulation Progressions in 4/4 (with Counterpoint) I & II* (pgs. 113-114) heighten the rhythmic tension–by shifting the LF/HH backbeat relative to each variation's timeline–and enhance the rhythmic flow–by adding a consistent comping pattern to each that contracts or expands throughout.

Practice Tips

It is recommended, in these modulation studies, to master each example individually, bar by bar, finding a centered and swinging time feel, at a variety of tempos, before segueing them together.

Examples of "Broken-Time" Ride Cymbal Phrasing

1. Open Drag in Root Position

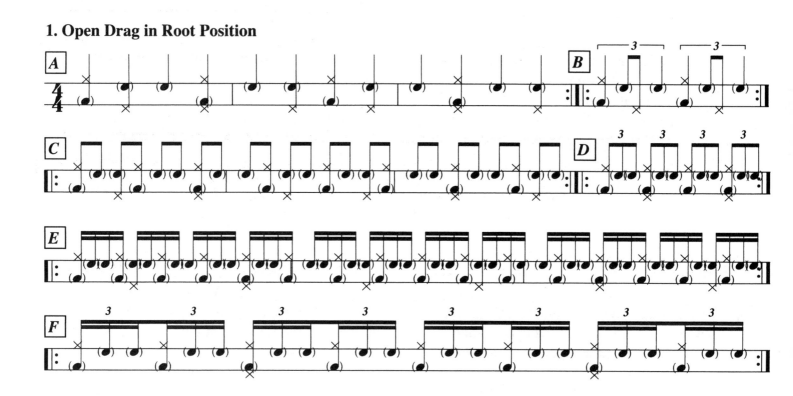

2. Open Drag in 1st Inversion

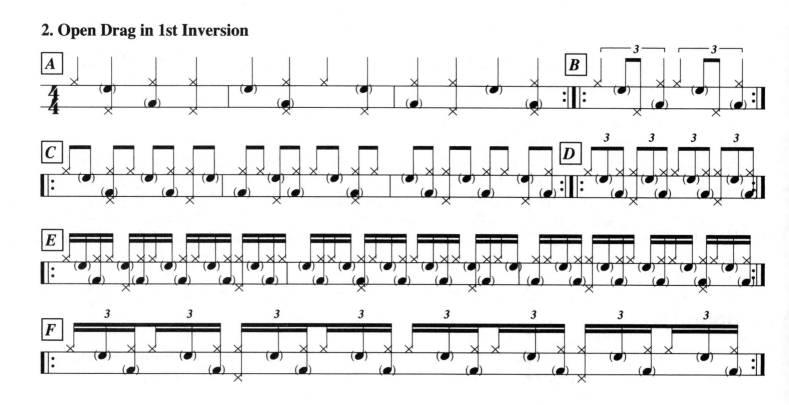

3. Four-Stroke Ruff in 1st Inversion

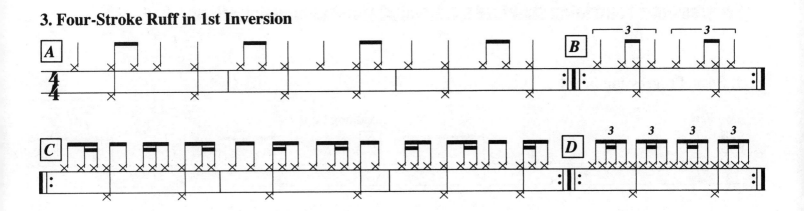

4. Four-Stroke Ruff in Root Position

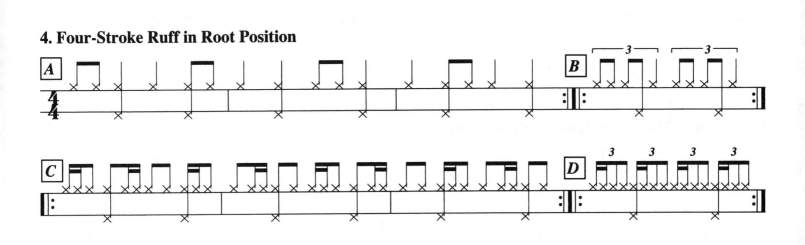

5. Five-Stroke Ruff in 2nd Inversion

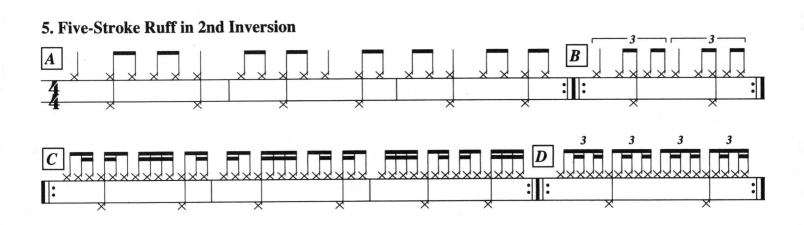

Progressions Combining Standard & Advanced Timekeeping Variations

1. Basic Progression in 4/4

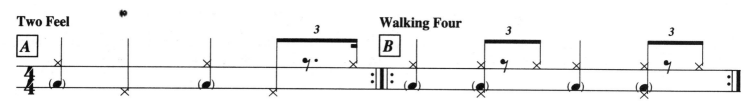

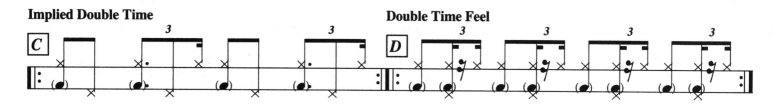

2. Implied Metric Modulation Progression in 3/4

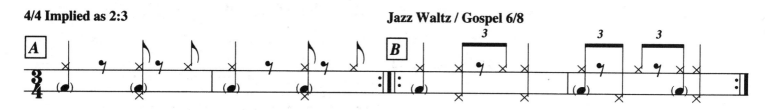

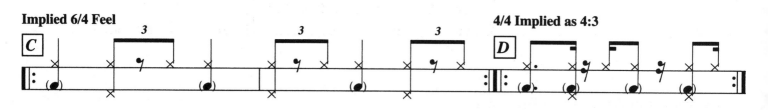

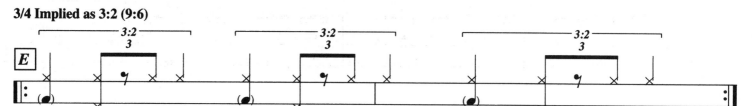

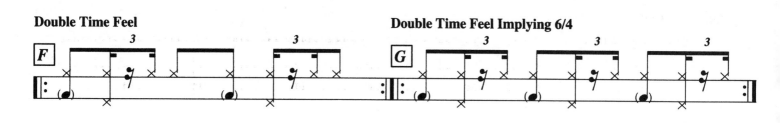

3. Implied Metric Modulation Progression in 4/4

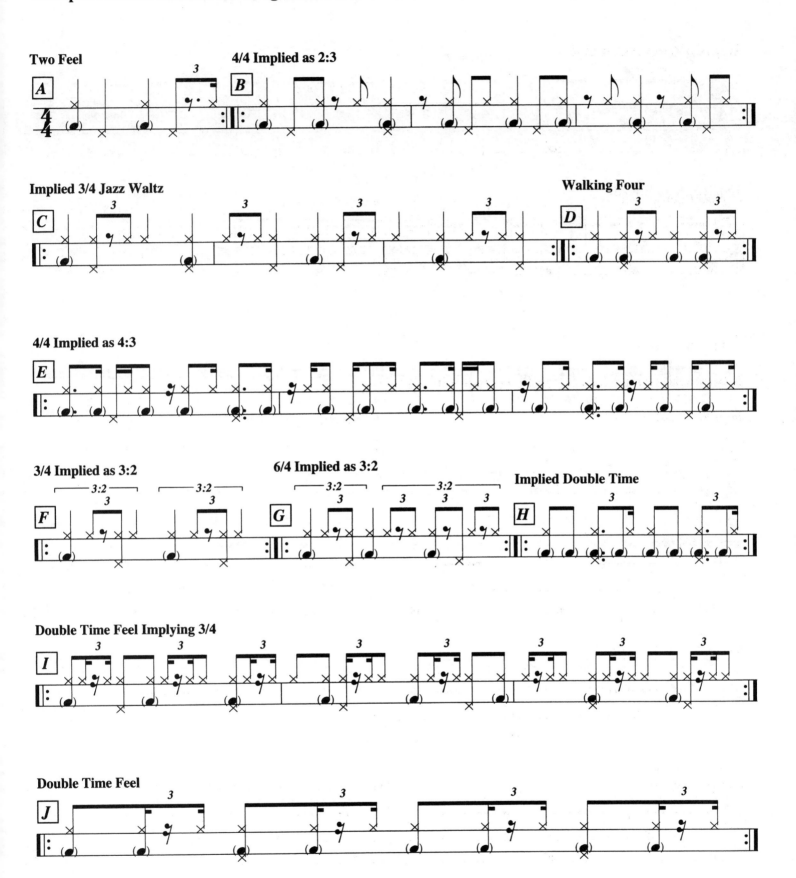

4. Advanced Implied Metric Modulation Progression in 4/4 (with Counterpoint) I

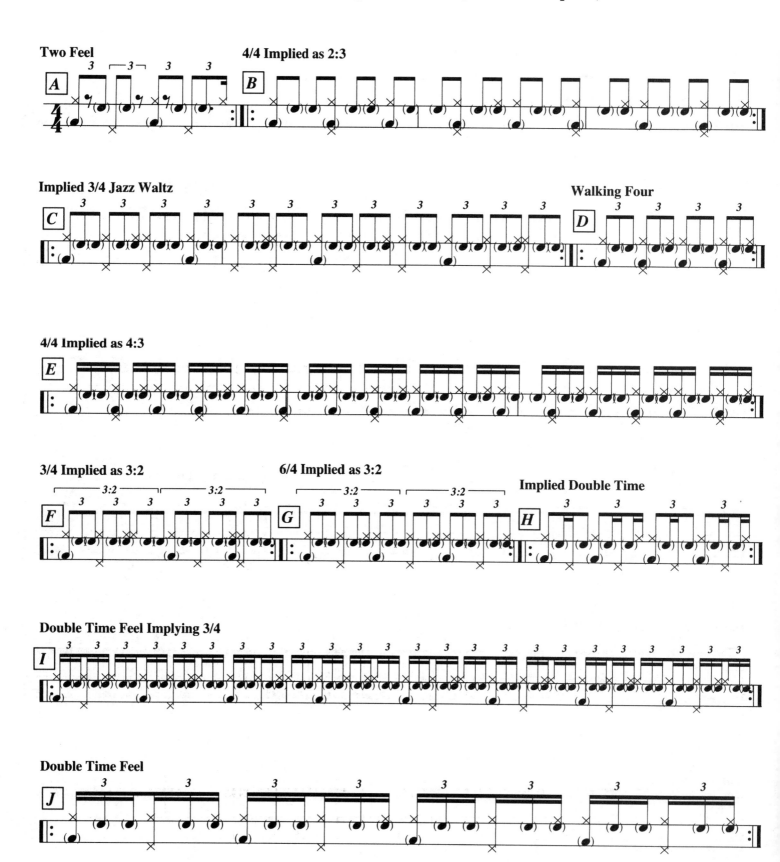

5. Advanced Implied Metric Modulation Progression in 4/4 (with Counterpoint) II

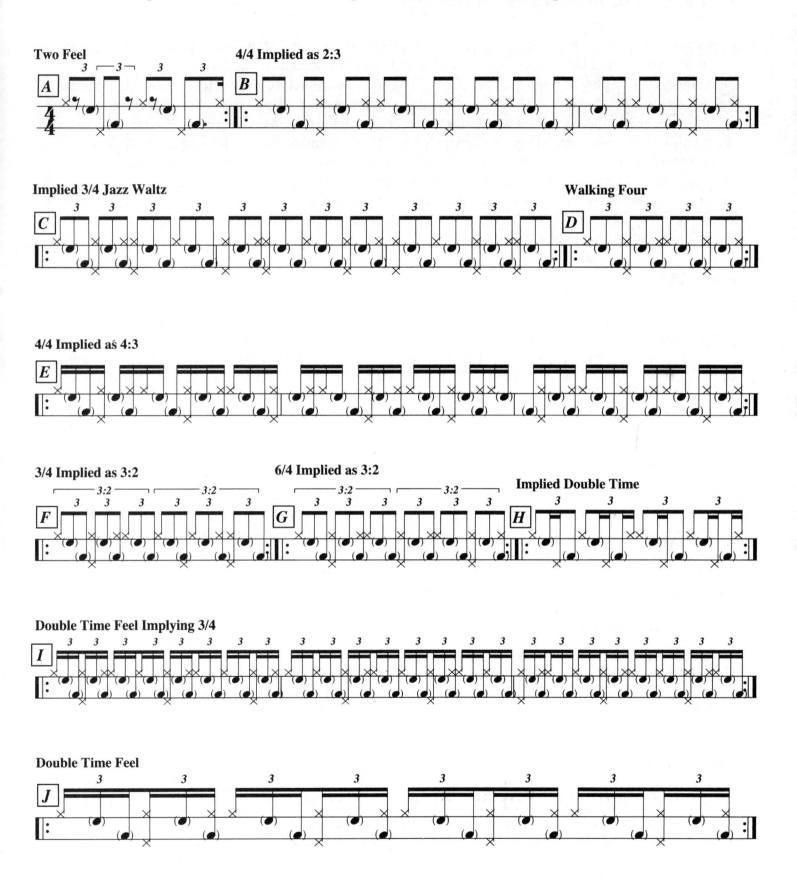

Part One: Interpreting Rudimental Studies

A message telegraphed across quiet African plains; the pulse of a celebratory village dance; the melody of tympani resonating in a concert hall; chanting and slapping skins on a Cuban street corner; a blisteringly fast display of logic and form in a hot New York nightclub; a theatrical explosion of sound, lights, and smoke, in an arena. The song of the drum solo has been sung in many ways over the centuries. Its evolution on the drumset touts syncopated cadences, "jungle drumming," improvised snare drum exhibition, song form adaptation, abstract "free-form" textures, double bass drum thunder, orchestrated compositions, and realized melodies, among its highlights. Whether improvised or arranged, mainstream or abstract, a solo requires composition (see *Ch. 1 ~ Interpretation Notes for Song Form Applications*, pg. 18) to communicate successfully with the listener. Vocabulary is essential for speaking in any language. In the language of the drumset, rudiments are commonly interpreted "around the kit" to establish such a vocabulary.

Application

How to interpret rudiments musically, to create communicative and interesting phrasing, is a subjective, personal art. Listening to the masters, in a variety of musical styles, is recommended to understand the variety of ways *one* rudimental idea can be interpreted. The applications presented here are not meant to be definitive but to serve as examples with which you can use your creative imagination to develop variations of your own. That being said, the interpretations presented are largely based on classic vocabulary for the drumset to provide a focal point and foundation for further exploration.

Practice Tips

Use a metronome for reference in executing each motive with the same attention to time and feeling that a good groove demands. Solos, whether played as fills, breaks, or in a long form, are exciting for both the player and listener. Nothing ruins the potential of a great fill, break, or solo faster than inattention to tempo as it is common for such efforts to rush, in particular, when the *space* of the tempo is not given the same consideration as the *notes*. The examples are applicable to a variety of musical styles. Experiment with the *nuances* of dynamics and articulation to determine the proper feeling you want to project.

Motives utilizing BD, SD and cymbal voicing *only* are presented in double-Swiss staff notation; those containing mounted and floor toms are presented in a five-line staff, so as to illustrate *visually* the melodic contour of the phrasing. The sticking, in these examples, is indicated underneath the first two measures of each timetable and remains consistent as the subdivisions double or triple, respectively. Bass drum "stickings" are interpretive–motives presented with "doubles" split between two bass drums can be played with just one, and vice versa. The drumset voicing used in this chapter was chosen to provide the most universal option for soloing applications in general and are as follows: BD (with double bass/pedal optional), SD, one mounted tom, one floor tom, and left and right side suspended cymbals. The *Counterpoint Ostinato Options for Feet* (pg. 26) offer accompaniment that can be applied to any of the examples. Remember that the modern-day drum or *trapset* (like the original "*contraption*") offers endless configurations. Use your imagination to adapt these examples to yours!

Long Roll Variations

1. Single-Stroke Roll I

2. Single-Stroke Roll II

3. Single-Stroke Roll III

L R L R L R L R L R L R L R L R L R L R L R L R L R L R L R L R L R L R

simile . . .

4. Double-Stroke Roll I

R R L L R R L L   R R L L R R L L R R L L   R R L L R R L L R R L L   simile . . .

5. Inverted Double-Stroke Roll

R L L R R L L R   R L L R R L L R R L L R R L L R R L L R R L L R   simile . . .

6. Double-Stroke Roll II

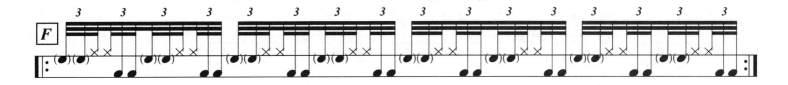

Paradiddle & Six-Stroke Roll Variations

1. Single Paradiddle I

R L R R L R L L   R L R R L R L L R L R R   L R L L R L R R L R L L

simile . . .

2. Single Paradiddle II

R L R R L R L L   R L R R L R L L   R L R R L R L L R L R R   L R L L R L R R L R L L

R L R R L R L L R L R R   L R L L R L R R L R L L   simile . . .

119

3. Double Paradiddle Variation

R L R L R R L R   L R L L R L R L   R R L R L R L L   R L R L R R L R L R L L

simile . . .

4. Six-Stroke Roll Variation

R L L R R L R L   L R R L R L L R   R L R L L R R L   R L L R R L R L L R R L

simile . . .

Flam & Drag Variations

1. Swiss Triplet Variation

L L R L L R R L L R R L L R R L L R R L L R R L L R R L L R R L L R R L L R R

L L R R L L R R L L R R L L R R

simile . . .

2. Open Drag Variation

Theme & Variation I: "Roundhouse" Motives Substituting Foot for Hand

1. Single-Stroke Roll I

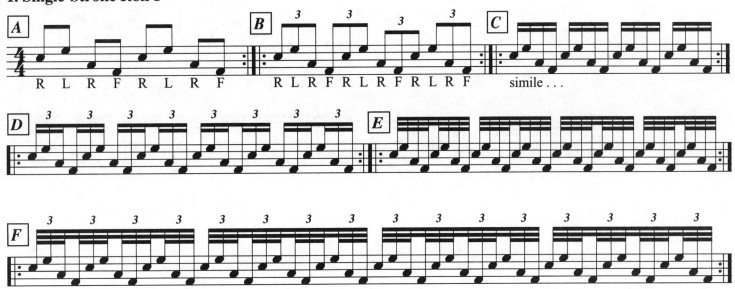

2. Single-Stroke Roll II

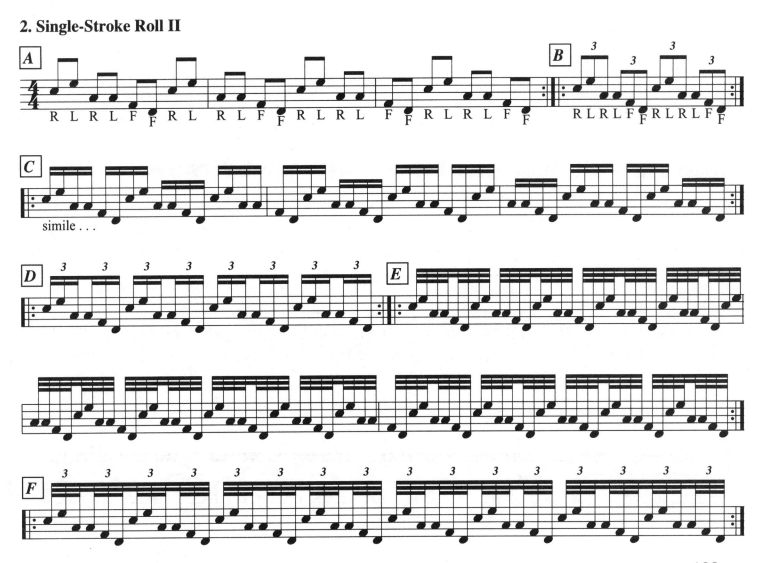

3. Single-Stroke Roll III

RLRLRLFF   RLRLRLFFRLRL RLFFRLRLRLFFF   simile . . .

Theme & Variation II: "Roundhouse" Motives w/"Broken" Rhythmic Phrasing

1. Four-Stroke Roll/Ratamacue w/Binary Phrasing

R L R F L L R L R F L L   R L R F L L R L R F L L L R L R F L L

2. Four-Stroke Roll w/Dotted Motive Phrasing

simile . . .

3. Four-Stroke Ruff in Root Position

simile . . .

Theme & Variation III: Related Motives/Voicing

1. Paradiddle-diddle

2. Flammed Five-Stroke Ruff

3. Swiss Triplet/Flam Drag "Blush-Da" Variation

125

Theme & Variation IV: Ergonomic Phrasing Progressions

1. Five-Stroke Ruff in Root Position

1.) R L R L R L R L R L R L R L R L R L R L   R L R L R L R L R L   R L R L R L R L R L

2.) R R L L R L L R R L R R L L R L L R R L   R R L L R L L R R L   R R L L R L L R R L

simile . . .

2. Long Roll/Hemiola Progression (Flam Tap Variation)

L R R R L L L R R R L L L R R R L L L R R R L L L R R R L L

L R R R L L L R R R L L L R R R L L L R R R L L

simile . . .

Common settings for drumset soloing include the *open solo*–typically a featured section of undetermined length within a song. It can also stand *free-form*–alone and independent of an ensemble setting. When *soloing over song form*, a "spontaneous melody" is created over the same measured chord progression cycle the other musicians use for their improvisation. *Soloing over a vamp* might be a groove provided by the rhythm section and also involve "kicks" or "hits" such as brass figures in a big-band setting or it might be an ostinato you provide to accompany yourself such as a "four-on-the-floor" bass drum or hi-hat backbeat on 2 & 4. The major benefit of a vamp is the space it allows you to use in your phrasing. A solo could simply be you alone playing an irresistible, hypnotic groove. Whatever the setting, you have the spotlight. Drum soloing concepts can vary as much as the settings they are applied to. Melodic, linear phrasing offers a conception fruitful for expanding our vocabulary beyond interpreting rudiments.

Application

The word *linear* is defined as consisting of, or resembling a line. This relates directly to the definition of a *melody*–a logical and memorable succession of tones combined with rhythm. A melody, at its root, is and can remain monophonic. *Linear drumming* refers to rhythms in which no voices on the drumset are played simultaneously. The *Melodic Linear Motive Studies* explored here combine the above ideas to produce phrasing that is linear in foundation and melodic through the considered arrangement of selected tones.

The *Melodic Triplet Progressions* (pg. 128) are another example of classic drumset vocabulary. The letter B motives are the "root rhythms" (see *Glossary of Terms*, pg. 135) of each variation. The *Root Position* progression is simply displaced through the *1st* and *2nd Inversions*. Reverse the sticking in the hands to create an inverse melodic contour for each variation. The studies *Adapting "Elastic Flurries"* (pg. 129) focus on phrases that change in velocity with the intent of providing an intense blur (or *flurry*) of sound that can create the illusion of *stretching* the motive. Exaggerate the accented vs. unaccented notes in *"Dropping Bombs I & II"* to maximize their effect. The *Soloing Applications* chapter concludes with a bit of musical fun in the *Cross-over Sticking Variations* (pg. 131). These progressions incorporate a visual act of showmanship in their execution as the RH "chases" the lead of the LH, clockwise around the drums. Observe the stickings carefully throughout. The variations are centered on one melodic cell, the "root rhythm" of which is found at letter B of Ex. 1, *Six-Note Motive*. This cell is embellished into the *Eight-Note Motive* by doubling the notes on the SD (see letter A of Ex. 2). The *Six-Note Motive* is then applied to a *Long Roll/Hemiola Progression* adding, through the inclusion of "broken rhythms," a sense of deconstruction to the motive beyond the compression and expansion of the *Standard Timetable* application (Ex. 1).

Practice Tips

Accompanying the motives with examples from the *Counterpoint Ostinato Options for Feet* (pg. 26), where appropriate transforms them into layered, polyphonic phrases providing a nice contrast when added to or subtracted from the linear, melodic flow.

Melodic Triplet Progressions

1. Root Position

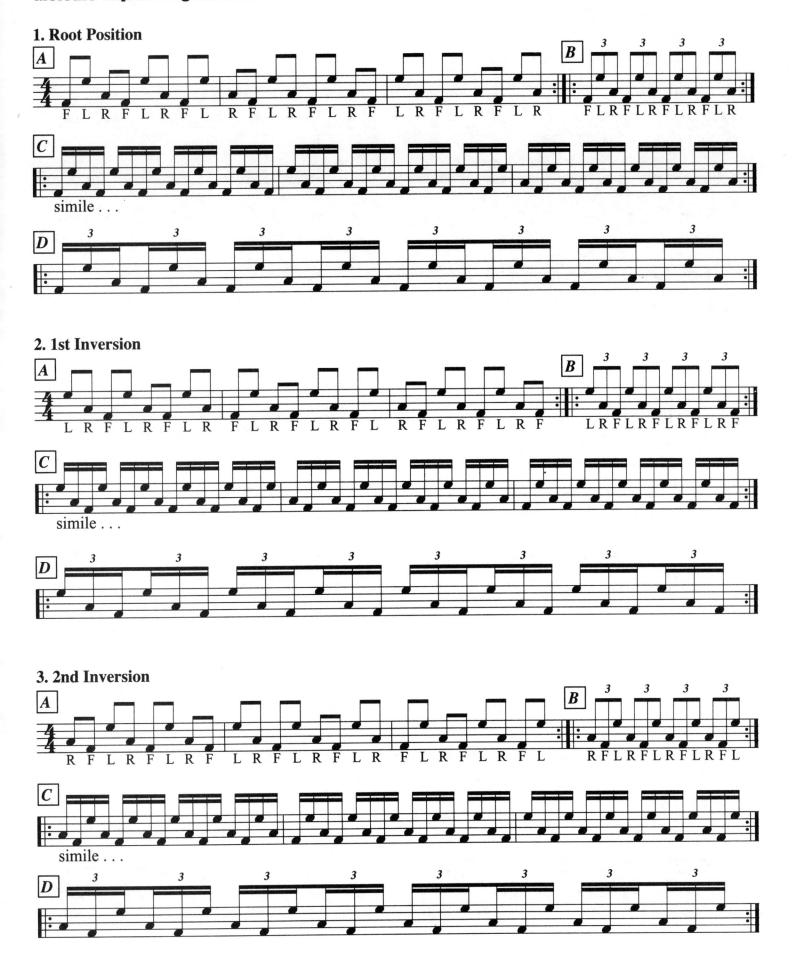

2. 1st Inversion

3. 2nd Inversion

Adapting "Elastic Flurries"

1. Expanding & Contracting Paradiddle Inversion Sticking

R L L R L R R L   R LL R L RR L R LL R L RR L   simile . . .

2. "Drop 2" (or "Extended Quad") Variation

3. "Dropping Bombs" I

F R F R F R F R   F R L F R L F R L F R L   F R L L F R L L F R L L F R L L

F R L L R L F R L L R L F R L L R L F R L L R L   F R L L R R L L F R L L R R L L F R L L R R L L F R L L R R L L

F R L L R R L L R R L L F R L L R R L L R R L L F R L L R R L L R R L L F R L L R R L L R R L L

4. "Dropping Bombs" II

R F R F R F R F   R L F R L F R L F R L F   R L F F R L F F R L F F R L F F

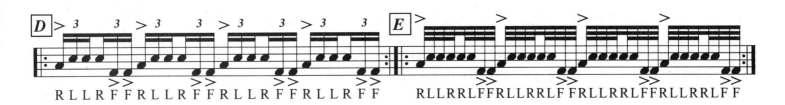

R L L R F F R L L R F F R L L R F F R L L R F F   R L L R R L F F R L L R R L F F R L L R R L F F R L L R R L F F

R L L R R L L R R L F F R L L R R L L R R L F F R L L R R L L R R L F F R L L R R L L R R L F F

Cross-over Sticking Variations

1. Six-Note Motive

L R L R L R L R L R L R L R L R L R L R L R L R

simile . . .

2. Eight-Note Motive

L R R L R L L R L R R L R L L R L R R L R L L R R L L R L R R L

simile . . .

3. Six-Note Motive in Long Roll/Hemiola Progression (Single-Stroke Variation)

The World Timetable Presented in Roundtable Form

The following page illustrates the *World Timetable* in *Roundtable Form* (see *Glossary of Terms*, pg. 135). *Volume II* of *Mastering the Tables of Time* introduces this more advanced timetable and explores the possibilities inherent to it by applying accents, rudiments, polyrhythms, grooves, and soloing applications to musical phrasing within its structure. A major difference between the *World Timetable* and *Standard Timetable* is its inclusion of asymmetric groupings of five, seven, and nine notes per beat. The *World Timetable*, within a simple meter framework, employs a *rhythm scale* that shifts its value groupings gradually, like the gears on a bike, from one to nine notes per beat as follows: quarter-notes, eighth-notes, eighth-note triplets, sixteenth-notes, quintuplets, sextuplets, octuplets, and nontuplets. While the numerical flow can continue, we will focus on these most common rhythmic groupings as applied to contemporary music. The goal is to be able to comfortably hear, anticipate and play musically through all of the note values while keeping steady time based on the quarter-note pulse.

Application

Begin by setting a metronome to a slow pulse of around 40 to 60 beats per minute. Try playing and singing the rhythms. Below each measure are syllables that correspond to the subdivisions. They are a simple version of a language of vocal percussion from south India called *konokol*. How to count the subdivisions is a subjective matter. Western music has a codified method for counting in compound meters but only an agreed structure in simple meter for counting duple subdivisions of quarter, eighth and sixteenth-notes, and nothing beyond that. Furthermore there is no agreement at all in how to count triplets in *any* subdivision. The eastern method of konokol offers an alternative with a consistency that is particularly helpful for "getting the feel" of the asymmetric groupings of five, seven, and nine, which are less familiar to some musicians.

Practice Tips

Beginning at letter A, the quarter-notes (or *downbeats*) use the syllable "*ta.*" The 8th notes (groups of *two*) at letter B, use "*ta-ka.*" 8th note triplets (groups of *three*) at letter C, use "*ta-ki-ta.*" 16th notes (groups of *four*) at letter D, use "*ta-ka-di-mi.*" In the simple form of konokol these four foundational syllable groupings are then combined to produce the sounds for the groupings that follow: groupings of *five* (letter E) use "*ta-ka-ta-ki-ta*" (or 2+3). Groupings of *six* (letter F) use "*ta-ki-ta-ta-ki-ta*" (or 3+3). Groupings of *seven* (letter G) use "*ta-ka-di-mi-ta-ki-ta*" (or 4+3). Groupings of *eight* (letter H) use "*ta-ka-di-mi-ta-ka-di-mi.*" (or 4+4), and the groupings of *nine* (letter I) use "*ta-ka-di-mi-ta-ka-ta-ki-ta*" (or 4+5). Letters J-Q simply repeat subdivisions A-I in reverse order (illustrating the *Roundtable Form* concept). This method is recommended to give you a mental common denominator for keeping the overall pulse steady. The verbalization is easy and helps internalize the subdivisions. You can then focus on the big picture, allowing you and the rhythm to better breathe, providing the foundation that we will build on in *Volume II*.

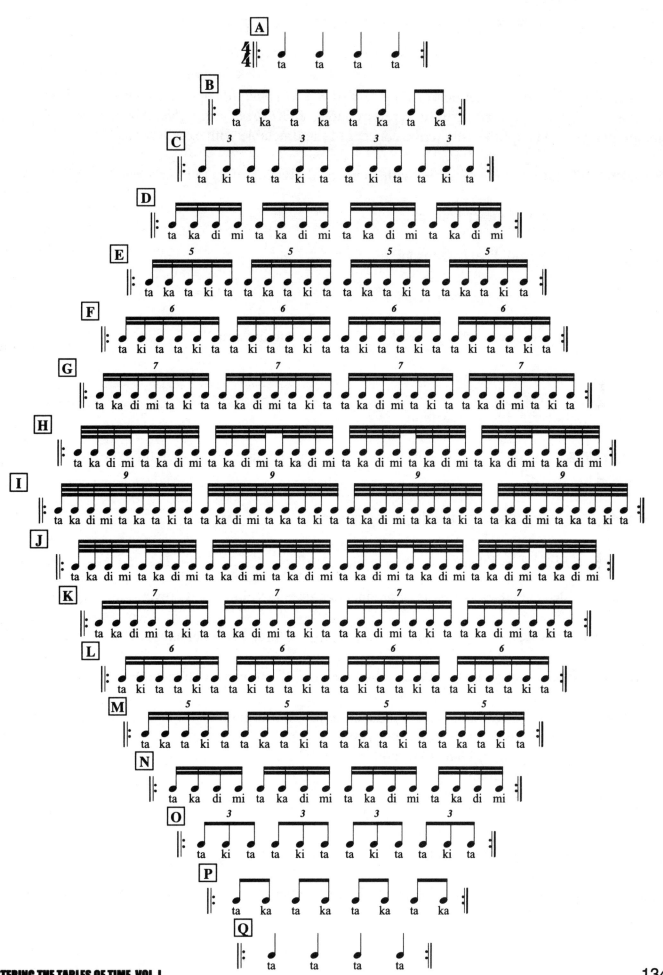

Glossary of Terms

The following is a list of terms unique or important to the text of this book.

Abstract Timetable ~ Any variation of a *Standard* or *World Timetable* operating outside of their definition, to achieve a desired purpose, is referred to as an *Abstract Timetable*. Abstraction in art is a common practice and applies easily to the concept of the timetable with excellent results.

Asymmetrical Meter ~ A time signature with an unequal division of its measures (such as 5/4 or 7/4).

ATT ~ Abbreviation for Abstract Timetable.

BF~ Abbreviation for Both Feet (in unison).

BH ~ Abbreviation for Both Hands (in unison).

Binary Phrasing ~ A motive with a pulse of two beats per subdivision.

BD ~ Abbreviation for Bass Drum.

BPM ~ Abbreviation for Beats Per Minute.

Compound Meter ~ A time signature divisible by three that contains more than three beats per bar (such as 6/8 or 6/4).

Crescendo ~ a gradual increase in volume and power.

Cym ~ Abbreviation for Cymbal

Diminuendo ~ (also called *decrescendo*) a gradual decrease in volume and power.

Dotted Motive Phrasing ~ A *ternary* motive with a pulse of three beats per subdivision.

Duple Subdivisions ~ Subdivisions divisible by 2 (such as 8th notes and 16th notes).

Dynamic Markings ~ musical notation for indicating how soft or loud to play:
  Pianississimo (ppp) = very, very soft
  Pianissimo (pp) = very soft; Piano (p) = soft
  Mezzo Piano (mp) = medium soft
  Mezzo forte (mf) = medium loud
  Forte (f) = loud
  Fortissimo (ff) = very loud
  Fortississimo (fff) = very, very loud

Etude ~ a composition designed for the development of a particular technique on a musical instrument.

Ghost Note ~ a tap stroke of light execution. Ghost notes are commonly played on the snare drum, providing a softer dynamic contrast to notes around it as with a flam, or the rhythmic undercurrent within a groove.

Hairpin ~ the term that describes the notational dynamic marking for playing either a crescendo (where the closed end of the hairpin in to the left and the open end is to the right), or a diminuendo (where the open end is to the left and the closed end is to the right).

Harmonic Coordination ~ Any two or more voices (limbs) played simultaneously on the drumset.

Hemiola ~ a rhythmic form of counterpoint that introduces a new meter on top of an existing one, creating a polyrhythm. Hemiola creates a rhythmic tension similar to the melodic tension of a leading tone and the harmonic tension of a suspended chord in how our ear craves a quick resolution when each musical device is employed.

HH ~ Abbreviation for Hi-Hat.

LF ~ Abbreviation for Left Foot.

L or LH ~ Abbreviation for Left Hand.

Melodic Coordination ~ Linear phrasing with only one voice (limb) played at a time on the drumset.

Metric Modulation ~ (or *implied metric modulation*) A *modulation* is a change of key signature A *metric* modulation then refers to a change of meter, or time signature, in which a new subdivision or polyrhythm is introduced to take on the role of the dominating pulse. This change of meter can be either actual, where the time signature in a composition changes, or *implied*, creating the feel of a new meter over the original pulse, which is retained throughout.

Ostinato ~ a clearly defined phrase repeating persistently, usually in the same voice or voices. On the drumset, ostinatos are typically executed with one or more limb while the remaining limbs play rhythmic counterpoint over them.

Polyrhythm ~ the coordination of two or more rhythms—each with their own metrically divided duration— into a simultaneous cycle. Polyrhythms can be defined in meter by choosing one rhythm to be the *foundation* and the other the *hemiola* over the foundation. For example 3:2 = three beats *over the space of* two beats. The second number defines the meter, the first number defines the *polymeter*. 2:3 = two beats *over the space of* three beats, or the exact opposite. The combination sounds the same either way but if you stress one pulse so as to imply it as a foundation and then switch the emphasis to stress the opposite pulse as the foundation you will execute what is called a metric modulation.

RF (or F) ~ Abbreviation for Right Foot.

R or RH ~ Abbreviation for Right Hand.

Rhythm Scale ~ See Timetable or Table of Time.

Root Position, 1ˢᵗ, 2ⁿᵈ and 3ʳᵈ Inversions ~ This is an abstract rhythmic conception with a structural relationship to harmonic theory. It employs a foundational rhythmic motive cycling within a timetable, beginning on, and perhaps also accenting, the downbeat of each measure. This timetable is labeled as being in *Root Position*. It is then followed by other timetables, each illustrating sequential *inversions* of all the possible permutations, or displacements, of that foundational rhythmic motive.

Think of the inversions as you would in a harmonic chord: *Root Position* outlines a chord with the tonic of the key on the bottom of the chord (1ˢᵗ, 3ʳᵈ, 5ᵗʰ). Applied to a rhythmic motive it would begin a timetable with its most common phrase or sticking. *1ˢᵗ Inversion* places the *second* note of a chord on the bottom, moving the first note to the top of the chord (3ʳᵈ, 5ᵗʰ, 1ˢᵗ). In our interpretation it would either move an accented (or otherwise ornamented) note to the *second* note in the sequence, or displace a specific sticking (beginning on the *second* note of the *Root Position* sticking, following in sequence and ending with the first note). The rotation sequence continues as above for *2ⁿᵈ* and *3ʳᵈ Inversions*. This concept will be referenced and used throughout the texts of *Volumes I* and *II*.

Root Rhythm ~ The foundational motive within a timetable that the examples around it are based on rhythmically and/or sticking-wise.

Roundtable Form ~ The term *Roundtable form* uses word play to define a *circular* approach to practicing the timetables throughout the book. As you play through each example, it is recommended that you repeat the example in reverse order–like an extended musical *arch* form.

It is a common problem among musicians to rush tempos when increasing subdivisions inside a quarter-note pulse and equally common to drag tempos when decreasing the subdivisions inside and outside the quarter-note pulse. The *Roundtable form* helps, when working with a metronome, to anticipate and eliminate this common problem through focused and repetitive playing. In the interest of saving space most of the timetables presented in this book will *not* be written out in this form but it is highly recommended you practice them in this fashion for best results in strengthening your "inner clock."

RTF ~ Abbreviation for Roundtable Form.

SD ~ Abbreviation for Snare Drum.

Simple Meter ~ A time signature in which each beat is divided into two equal components (such as 2/2 or 2/4).

Standard Timetable ~ The term *Standard Timetable* is a play on words borrowing from the world's division into different time zones, a standard zone being a commonly accepted one. The *Standard Timetable* focuses on duple and triple subdivisions, expanding around or contracting inside a simple meter quarter-note pulse, as they are the most commonly used in popular music.

STT ~ Abbreviation for Standard Timetable.

Syncopation ~ Shifting the accent from a standard *strong* beat (like a downbeat) to one that is normally *weak* (like an upbeat) or unexpected. Contrast, for example, the accented pulse of a European 2/4 march rhythm (emphasizing the *downbeat* as "**1**-&-**2**-&" to keep troops marching together in a unified formation), with the accented pulse of an American 2/4 gospel church rhythm (stressing the *upbeat* as "1-**&**-2-**&**" when the congregation sings and claps their hands). The latter pulse is a syncopated one.

Timeline ~ the length of a motive or groove as defined not by the bars of the time signature it is played within or over but rather by the number of notes in its subdivision.

Time Signature ~ a fraction placed at the beginning of a piece of music and anywhere within where the meter or tempo of the piece might change. Top number of the fraction indicates the number of beats in the bar or measure and the bottom number defines which subdivision of a note receives the count of one beat. 2/4, 3/4, 4/4, 5/4, 6/4, 7/4, 8/8, 12/8 and 8/16 are examples of different time signatures explored in this book.

Timetable or Table of Time ~ These terms have their origins in world time zone conversion and organizing train travel schedules. Applied to the musical art, they outline an ordered progression of subdivisions within a common meter or pulse. This progression is also known as the *Rhythm Scale*.

Triple Subdivisions ~ Subdivisions divisible by 3 (such as 8th note triplets and 16th note triplets).

TT ~ Abbreviation for Timetable.

World Timetable ~ The term *World Timetable* is another play on words from the world's division into different time zones, with the world clock being the mainframe for all of them. The *World Timetable* weaves asymmetric subdivisions of five, seven, and nine notes into a progressive sequence among the standard duple and triple ones found inside a simple meter quarter-note pulse. These subdivisions are commonly used in music of the world from countries including Africa, India, Greece and Turkey.

WTT ~ Abbreviation for World Timetable.

V.S. ~ (*Volti Subito*) turn the page quickly (or proceed very suddenly) to the next measure.

Selected Media for Further Study

The following is a selected listing of recommended media for broadening your horizons in the musical directions explored in *Mastering the Tables of Time, Volume I*. Some may be out of print but, in this day and age, that doesn't mean you can't find them if you're resourceful! We live in a time where access to information is quicker ever before. A lot of inspiring material is at your fingertips. Check it all out. Feed your mind, inspire yourself, and get out and play! It's the best way to learn of all.

ALAN DAWSON METHOD

4-Way Coordination, Marvin Dahlgren & Elliot Fine (Henry Adler, Inc.); *Stick Control*, George L. Stone (G.B. Stone, Inc.); *Progressive Steps to Syncopation for the Modern Drummer*, Ted Reed (Ted Reed, Inc); *Alan Dawson Drum Method, Volumes 1 & 2*, Osami Mizuno, w/Steve Smith–Vol. 2 (Osami Office); *The Drummer's Complete Vocabulary as taught by Alan Dawson*, John Ramsay (Warner Bros.).

BACKBEAT STUDIES

The Groove is Here, Steve Jordan (Rittor Music); *The Ultimate Realistic Rock Drum Method*, Carmine Appice (Alfred Music); *Complete Text for the Rock and Roll Drummer*, Marvin Dahlgren & Elliot Fine (Henry Adler, Inc.); *Future Sounds*, David Garibaldi (Alfred Music); *Give the Drummers Some!/The Great Drummers of R&B, Funk & Soul*, Jim Payne (Mel Bay, Inc); *Take It to the Street*, Stanton Moore (Carl Fischer); *Jungle Drum 'n' Bass for the Acoustic Drumset*, Johnny Rabb (Warner Bros.).

CONCEPTUAL INFORMATION

Drum Wisdom, Bob Moses (Modern Drummer Publications), *The Drum Perspective*, Peter Erskine (Hal Leonard); *Time Awareness for All Musicians*, Peter Erskine (Alfred Music); *How Not to Play the Drums (Not for Drummers Only)*, Charli Persip (Second Floor Music); *Big Time*, Billy Ward (Hal Leonard).

COORDINATION/TECHNIQUE

Master Studies I & II, Joe Morello (Modern Drummer Publications); *Bass Drum Control*, Colin Bailey (Hal Leonard); *Double Bass Drumming*, Joe Franco (DC Publications); *Single Stroke Rolls and The Open/Close Technique,* Gordy Knudtson (GK Music); *Snare Drum & Drumset Techniques*, Gordy Knudtson (GK Music); *Hi-Hat Control*, Marvin Dahlgren (M. Dahlgren, Inc.); *Drumset Technique/History of the U.S. Beat*, Steve Smith (Hudson Music); *The Freehand Technique*, Johnny Rabb (J. Rabb Publications); *Secret Weapons for the Modern Drummer*, JoJo Mayer (Hudson LTD).

JAZZ STUDIES

Advanced Techniques for the Modern Drummer, Jim Chapin (J.Chapin, Inc); *The Art of Modern Jazz Drumming*, Jack DeJohnette & Charlie Perry (DC Publications); *Jazz Methodology in Drum Music (In & Out of Meter)*, Andrew Cyrille (Alchemy Pictures); *Jazz Drumming*, Billy Hart (Advance Music); *New Orleans Jazz and Second Line Drumming*, Herlin Riley & Johnny Vidacovich (Warner Bros.); *Art Blakey's Jazz Messages*, John Ramsay (Warner Bros.); *Inside Buddy Rich*, Jim Nesbitt w/Buddy Rich (Kendor Music); *Musical Time*, Ed Soph (Carl Fischer); *The Art of Bop Drumming/Beyond Bop Drumming*, John Riley (Manhattan Music); *Brush Artistry*, Philly Joe Jones (Premier); *The Art of Playing with Brushes*, Adam Nussbaum, Steve Smith, Joe Morello, Charlie Persip, Eddie Locke, Billy Hart, Ben Riley and more (Hudson Music).

MULTI-PURPOSE RESOURCES

UpClose/In Session, Steve Gadd (DCI), *The New Breed*, Gary Chester (Modern Drummer Publications); *Drum Styles and Independence Techniques*, Gordy Knudtson (GK Music); *Moves & Grooves for Drumset*, Elliot Fine (Kjos Music); *Solo Drums*, Terry Bozzio (Warner Bros.*); The Erskine Method for Drumset*, Peter Erskine (Alfred Music); *Time, Taste Technique & Timbre*, Ed Shaughnessy & Clem DeRosa (Hal Leonard), *The Drumset Soloist*, Steve Houghton (Warner Bros).

READING DEVELOPMENT

Accent on Accents, Books 1 & 2, Elliot Fine & Marvin Dahlgren (Henry Adler, Inc.); *Reading Text for Drummers*, Paul Stueber, Jess Wheeler, David Stanoch, Gordy Knudtson (GK Music); *Rhythm & Accents for Drummers*, Gordy Knudtson (GK Music); *Modern Rudimental Swing Solos for the Advanced Drummer*, Charles S. Wilcoxon (C.S.W. Inc); *Portraits in Rhythm*, Anthony Cirone (Warner Bros.); *Rhythmic Illusions*, Gavin Harrison (Warner Bros.); *It's Time for the Big Band Drummer*, Mel Lewis & Clem DeRosa (Kendor Music); *Big, Bad & Beautiful–Drumset Method Book & Playalong & Practice Kit*, Roy Burns (1st Place Music); *Their Time Was the Greatest*, Louie Bellson (Warner Bros.).

Bonus Supplement Page from the FREE Online Audio/Video Companion

The following is a sample supplemental page expanding on chapter studies found throughout the book.

This page and many more can be found online in the FREE Audio/Video Companion for *Mastering the Tables of Time* at www.rhythmelodic.com, as described in detail on pg.viii. Be sure to check it out!

2, 3, & 4-Way Coordination Supplement for Chapters 1-5
Coordination Options for Two-Voice Sticking Combinations

Here is a listing of 2, 3 and 4-Way Coordination options applicable to the interpretation of various two-voice "sticking" combinations found throughout Chapters 1-5. Alternate "sticking"combinations are indicated directly below each original one.

KEY: RH = Right Hand; LH = Left Hand; RF = Right Foot; LF = Left Foot; BH = Both Hands; BF = Both Feet; RR = Right Limbs; LL = Left Limbs.

2-Way	3-Way		4-Way
1. RH/LH	1. RH/LL	7. RR/LH	1. RR/LL
LH/RH	LL/RH	LH/RR	LL/RR
2. RF/LF	2. LH/RR	8. RR/LF	2. BH/BF
LF/RF	RR/LH	LF/RR	BF/BH
3. RH/LF	3. RH/BF	9. LL/RH	3. RH+LF/LH+RF
LF/RH	BF/RH	RH/LL	LH+RF/RH+LF
4. LH/RF	4. LH/BF	10. LL/RF	
RF/LH	BF/LH	RF/LL	
5. RH/RF	5. BH/RF	11. RH+LF/LH	
RF/RH	RF/BH	LH/RF+LH	
6. LH/LF	6. BH/LF	12. LH+RF/RH	
LF/LH	LF/BH	RH/LH+RF	